8 Models of Ethnic Ministry

Outreach Alive!

Models *of* Ethnic Ministry

Outreach Alive!

**Edited by
Robert H. King**

CONCORDIA PUBLISHING HOUSE • SAINT LOUIS

Copyright © 2006 Concordia Publishing House
3558 S. Jefferson Ave., St. Louis, MO 63118-3968
1-800-325-3040 • www.cph.org

Maufactured in the United States of America

Library of Congress Cataloging-in-Publication Data

Eight models of ethnic ministry: outreach alive! / edited by Robert H. King
        p. cm.
ISBN 0-7586-1297-4
1. Mission—Case studies. 2. Ethnic relations—Case studies. King, Robert
H., 1922-

BV2063.E39 2006
266′.4132208—dc22

2006019595

1 2 3 4 5 6 7 8 9 10   15 14 13 12 11 10 09 08 07 06

Contents

CONTRIBUTORS

STEVE COHEN—founder of the Apple of His Eye Mission Society, St. Louis, Missouri

CLARK GIES—executive director of the Council for Lutheran American Indian Ministry, Fairfax, South Dakota

ROOSEVELT GRAY—director of missions for the Michigan District of The Lutheran Church—Missouri Synod, Ann Arbor, Michigan

MARK JUNKANS—executive director of LINC-Houston, Houston, Texas

KHURRAM KHAN—executive director of People of the Book Lutheran Outreach, Dearborn Heights, Michigan

SHIU MING LAU—formerly pastor of Light of Christ Lutheran Mission, St. Louis, Missouri, is now pastor of Lutheran Church of the Holy Spirit, San Francisco, California

YOHANNES MENGSTEAB—director for National Mission Team of The Lutheran Church—Missouri Synod, St. Louis, Missouri

S. T. WILLIAMS—pastor, St. Paul Lutheran Church, Los Angeles, California

ACKNOWLEDGMENTS

May God be praised for the faithful persons who helped graciously in the preparation of this anthology. We express heartfelt thanks for the superb presentations of the eight contributors who gave the book its singular uniqueness: Living examples of contemporary ethnic ministry.

I offer sincere appreciation to the Rev. Paul McCain for listening to my initial thoughts of writing an anthology on ethnic ministries. Dr. Paul Maier's encouragement afforded incentive to make this unusual contribution to the Lord's church.

Students in English classes have heard their teachers explain how we learn through writing. Thus I am immeasurably thankful to Concordia Seminary, St. Louis, for asking me to design and teach two different courses on ethnic ministries. Developing and teaching the courses immeasurably increased my knowledge of ministries in ethnic contexts. A decade of full course enrollment and excellent evaluations were encouraging as I made notes and plans for each new term. Needless to say, the coursework experiences had a great impact on my conceptualization of this anthology.

Dr. Jean King, my faithful wife of fifty-six years, receives my hearty appreciation for her tireless understanding, capable assistance, insightful skills, and experience with literature in helping with the editing of the manuscript. Moreover, I wish to express heartfelt thanks to our son, Roger, for his expert technology skills in organizing and formatting the final manuscript for publication.

PREFACE

This anthology provides models of ethnic ministry within a Lutheran theological perspective for use by church leaders in planning their own programs. The eight leaders offer ideas, insights, techniques, and strategies for ethnic ministries, and two final chapters provide practical application.

Major observations expected to occur in this project are population diversities, culture differences, language concerns, coping with adverse conditions, and various religious beliefs and practices. An important observation is the U.S. population of approximately 295 million people with subpopulations of diverse identities. Major components are U.S. citizens, immigrants, and displaced persons. The makeup of a once predominantly Anglo population is changing with Black, Hispanic, Chinese, Korean, Hmong, African immigrant, Vietnamese, Japanese, Asian Indian, Ethiopian, etc. They are here among us to enrich, challenge, and change us.[1]

Cultures may vary in different ethnic communities and also serve as a base for their everyday lives and values. There are numerous definitions for culture, but the one selected for this purpose includes habits and customs, the way people develop, the way people cope with living and changing. With habits and customs, observable behaviors are to be noticed. People develop culture, it is not innate and genetic. People are not born with a culture. They are born into culture. Cultural norms tend to make life more rational and organized. Culture is changeable for most desirable cultural behaviors. Micro-cultures are experienced by people's personal

[1] *Missionary to Missionary News Letter* (March 20, 2001), 10.3.

satisfactions. These specific cultures are practical for people who are mobile for change to a better life.

Most non-English speaking cultural groups usually communicate in their native languages or use other languages learned and/or accepted in the geographic environment in which they live. The world has 4,445 languages spoken by 22,000 people groups representing 220 countries (LCMS Presidential Report 1988–89). Public media and other means of communication disclose repeatedly that the world is now the cosmic community. With the United States as a segment of this cosmic community, millions in this country represent multitudinous languages spoken by thousands of people from various countries and islands of the world.

Life-coping skills are required for satisfying and productive living in the United States. Life-coping conditions are not always found easy by ethnic minorities in a society controlled by an ethnic majority. Moreover, persons need technological skills and/or academic competencies for good paying jobs. Communicative skills in English and personalities that connect with employers and fellow employees are essential. Some colleges realize the majority of their students need a larger picture of the world in order to do their best work. An example is Montgomery College in suburban Washington DC, which reported one-third of 22,000 students were non-U.S. citizens from 175 countries.[2]

Religion is a huge concern with numerous thousands of ethnic persons migrating into the United States. This makes it a major mission field. No longer do missionaries have to leave this country to fulfill the mission call because the greatest mission field is here with its rapidly increasing need of ministry to ethnic persons joining the millions of American citizens. A recent report estimates that 150 million persons in the United States are without the saving love of Jesus for forgiveness of sin and deliverance from death and the devil. There are all sorts and conditions of people who are human beings with one Creator. Many people are like pilgrims, wandering in a vast desert, not knowing where they are going, people who want to go to heaven, but don't know the way.

People who are lost.

People claiming to have no kind of religion.

People who say God is whatever they perceive Him to be.

---

[2] *USA Today* (April 11, 2005).

People who have heard of Christ but do not know Him as Savior.

People whose God is their money, accomplishment, or popularity.

The fools who say, "There is no God" (Psalm 14:1).

These people are without the divine pillars of Lutheran theology that offer a solid base on which to build their spiritual lives. The divine pillars are:

Sola Scriptura—The inspired Word of God is the only norm for faith and practice (2 Timothy 3:16–17);

Sola Gratia—Salvation is by grace alone for Christ's sake (Ephesians 2:8–9); and

Sola Fide—Through faith alone in Christ as the one and only Savior (Romans 1:17; Acts 4:12).

These pillars are subscribed to by biblical doctrines and historical confessions. Evidence is undeniably established that all people have spiritual needs: "[A]ll have sinned and fall short of the glory of God" (Romans 3:23). Thus all people need to be reconciled to God through faith in Jesus Christ who affirms: "I am the way, and the truth, and the life. No one comes to the Father except through Me" (John 14:6).

The uniqueness of this book is eight pastoral practitioners serving eight groups of minorities in geographic locales throughout the United States and the Caribbean. The leaders take under consideration who their ethnic groups are, their characteristics, cultures, life situations, and that they are small ethnic minorities in a mammoth number-one world society. There are hundreds of ethnic groups in the United States, but the groups in this study are singled out and selected because their leaders are called or appointed by church officials or church entities to share the Word of God with them. As ministers deliver God's Word with the gracious power of the Holy Spirit in understandable languages and in the meaningful contexts of people's cultures, we have faith that God will change the course of the lives of ethnic minorities who are without Christ's salvation.

Rev. Robert H. King, Ph.D.
Fourth Vice-President
The Lutheran Church—Missouri Synod
St. Louis, Missouri

Eight Models of Ethnic Ministry

Outreach Ministry
to Jewish Americans

Steve Cohen
founder of Apple of His Eye Mission Society, St. Louis, Missouri

Now the LORD had said to Abram, "Go from your country and your kindred and your father's house to the land that I will show you. And I will make of you a great nation, and I will bless you and make your name great, so that you will be a blessing. I will bless those who bless you, and him who dishonors you I will curse, and in you all the families of the earth shall be blessed." (Genesis 12:1–3)

Thus says the LORD, who gives the sun for light by day and the fixed order of the moon and the stars for light by night, who stirs up the sea so that its waves roar—the LORD of hosts is His name: "If this fixed order departs from before Me, declares the LORD, then shall the offspring of Israel cease from being a nation before Me forever." Thus says the LORD: "If the heavens above can be measured, and the foundations of the earth below can be explored, then I will cast off all the offspring of Israel for all that they have done, declares the LORD." (Jeremiah 31:35–37)

My people, the Jewish people, are the descendants of Abraham, Isaac, and Jacob. They are God's covenant people who were called into a relationship with the Lord for a very specific purpose: to be a light to the nations. Israel was God's chosen people who were to declare His glory to the world. But God's covenant with Abraham never granted automatic salvation. Y'shua, the Messiah, came according to the Law (*Torah*), the Prophets (*Nevi'im*), and the Writings (*Ketuvim*) to redeem all mankind through His suffering, death, and resurrection. He is the only way to salvation (John 14:6; Acts 4:12), which was given to the Jews first (Romans 1:16).

Over the last four thousand years, God has superintended the survival of the Jewish people, though Hamans, Herods, and Husseins have sought their annihilation. Today, there are approximately thirteen million Jews worldwide. Of that number, about six million reside in the United States, and around five million live in Israel. Conservative missiologists guesstimate that in North America about one-tenth of 1 percent (around sixty thousand) confess Y'shua as Savior. A survey taken by Dr. Erv Kolb in the 1980s revealed that approximately 2 percent of those were members of The Lutheran Church—Missouri Synod (LCMS) congregations. According to Dr. Kolb, more Jewish believers attended Baptist or Pentecostal churches, primarily because of their eschatology that predicts Israel's future salvation (Romans 11:24–26).

In the United States, Jewish people who have not yet confessed Y'shua fall into four broad groupings: Orthodox, Conservative, Reform, and Reconstructionist. Approximately 14 percent of nonbelieving Jews claim to be Orthodox, 23 percent Conservative, 35 percent Reform, and less than 3 percent Reconstructionist.

Jewish views of the Bible, God, sin, eternal life, and the Messiah differ widely from person to person. Even if one claims to be part of a specific branch of Judaism, that does not mean someone can presume to have an understanding of his or her theological views; we must ask each person individually what he or she believes in order to speak wisely about the role of God and the Bible and sending Messiah for our sins.

ORTHODOX JUDAISM

Historically, there was no such thing as Jewish Orthodoxy; all Jewish practice was more or less the same. Today, the term "Orthodox" is used primarily in North America. Elsewhere, the distinction is primarily between the "more observant" and the "less observant." The specific term "Orthodox Judaism" is of rather recent origin and is used more as a generic term to differentiate the Jewish movements that follow traditional practices from the Jewish movements that are considered more "liberal."

Orthodox Judaism claims to be the movement that continues the beliefs and practices of biblical Judaism as accepted by the Jewish nation at

Mount Sinai with the giving of both the Oral and Written Law. These were codified during following generations in a dynamic process that continues to this day.

Orthodox Judaism is not a singular movement with a monolithic governing body. It is an amalgamation of many different movements that adhere to common principles. Generally, Orthodox movements share similar observances and beliefs but differ in the details. Orthodox movements also hold a wide spectrum of opinions toward modern culture and toward the modern state of Israel. All of Orthodox Judaism shares one common feature: a dedication to Law (Torah), both Written and Oral.

Orthodox Theology

For the Orthodox, the term "Torah" (law) refers to the "Written Torah" as interpreted by the "Oral Torah." The Oral Torah was originally interpreted by the medieval commentators and was eventually codified in Rabbi Joseph Karo's work, *Shulkhan Arukh* (code of Jewish Law). In Orthodox Judaism, the Written and Oral Torah are of divine origin and were given simultaneously to Moses on Mount Sinai.

To handle practical questions, Orthodox authorities use the process called *Halakah*, a system of legal reasoning and interpretation described in the Oral Torah. The goal is determining how best to live in accordance with God's will. In this way, Orthodoxy evolves to meet the demands of the times.

Orthodox Judaism encourages its members to question what God requires of us. Orthodox Jews respond to these questions systematically. Among the major Jewish movements, only Orthodoxy has preserved the "mystical" elements of Jewish theology, mainly within Chasidism and also in many *yeshivot* (Rabbinic seminaries), both Ashkenazi (Eastern European) and Sephardi (Spanish emphasis).

CONSERVATIVE JUDAISM

Conservative Judaism springs from an attempt to "conserve" Jewish traditions in the United States. The founders of the Conservative movement held that Orthodox and Reform Judaism would not survive in America.

Conservative Judaism attempts to combine an affirmative attitude toward current culture, an acceptance of critical scholarship pertaining to Judaism's sacred texts, as well as a commitment to Jewish observance.

Attitude toward *Halakah*

Recall that the term *Halakah* refers to a system of legal reasoning and interpretation described in the Oral Torah. The central halakhic authority of the movement is the Committee on Jewish Law and Standards (CJLS). The CJLS often sets out more than one acceptable position on an issue. In such a case, the rabbi of the congregation is free to choose from the range of acceptable positions (or none of them), and his congregation is expected to abide by his choice.

Many observers get the wrong idea about Conservative Judaism as being like Reform Judaism, except with more Hebrew in its liturgy. They believe that if one simply goes to a Conservative synagogue, then one is a Conservative Jew. This, of course, is not true. The movement's leadership, like many religious leaders, is deeply concerned with whether or not the next generation of Conservative Jews will have the commitment to lead an authentic Jewish lifestyle.

Conservative Theology

Conservative Judaism holds that the laws of the Torah and Talmud are of divine origin, but the tradition also recognizes the human element in the Torah and Talmud. Conservative Judaism acknowledges the legitimacy of modern scientific biblical criticism, claiming that Jewish writings reflect the influence of other cultures.

The majority of conservative Jews, but not all in this movement, believes that God is real and that God's will is made known to humanity through revelation.

REFORM JUDAISM

One of the main beliefs of Reform Judaism is the independence of the individual. A Reform Jew can decide whether to subscribe to this particular belief or to that particular practice.

The Reform movement springs from the Enlightenment era in which there is a move away from the spiritual or perhaps better said the supernatural, reducing most things to the scientific and observable.

The scriptures are not considered as divine in origin but man-made. Many rabbis in the Jewish Reform movement question the very existence of God. Part of this comes from the post-Holocaust era, as many wonder where God was during the destruction of six million Jewish people.

Early in my missionary career, a member of the Jewish Defense League, a militant Jewish group, and I were awaiting the arrival of an airplane at John F. Kennedy airport in New York during a snowstorm. We had a lengthy conversation, but when it came to understanding God, he told me point-blank that he had put God on trial and now to him God was dead as a result of forsaking our people.

My family grew up in the Reform movement. One of the tradition's important tenets was to make this world a better place through the deeds we are able to perform. At the same time, Reform Judaism does not believe in an afterlife. There is here and now, and when one dies, that is the end. This is in denial of what the Bible teaches in Daniel 12:2—that there will be a resurrection, some to everlasting life, others to everlasting torment.

The Reform movement is not looking for a personal Messiah, just a Messianic Age, akin to the age of Aquarius, a time of world peace brought on by our own efforts to rectify the wrongs by doing good.

Reconstructionism

Reconstructionist Jews define Judaism as the evolving religious group of Jewish people. The Jewish people share both historical memory and destiny. Judaism includes a responsibility to an ancient homeland and language. They impart a love for Jewish culture, Jewish morality, and Jewish philosophy.

Judaism has changed over the centuries. The faith of the ancient Israelites in the days of Solomon's Temple was not the same as that of the early rabbis. And neither of those faiths was the same as that of our more recent European ancestors. Each generation of Jews has helped the evolution of faith and traditions.

For Reconstructionist Jews, Judaism is the means by which Jews conduct their search for ultimate meaning in life. Reconstructionists believe that each Jew must find a unique path to the divine. They believe in a God who inhabits this world and especially the human heart. God is found when Jews study and when they work to foster morality and social justice.

For purposes of personal evangelism today, Christians must not stereotype Jewish people simply because they claim to be part of one "movement" or another. Asking pertinent questions will assist Christians in learning about the hopes and aspirations for Jewish life, as well as a Jewish person's thoughts on eternal life and the Messiah. The Reform and Reconstructionist movements have given up on a personal Messiah coming and have distanced themselves from taking the Bible literally when it comes to eternal life. For them, life ends at death.

THE APPLE OF HIS EYE AND JEWISH MISSIONS

Jewish missions are different from missions to other groups. If you wanted to reach a tribe in Africa, for instance, you could mount an agricultural, medical, literacy, or educational mission, and then piggyback the Gospel along with the services rendered. Not so with my people. They have taken a desert and made it bloom, they are on the forefront of medical and scientific advances, and they are highly literate. So piggybacking is not an option.

Yet despite their intellectual prowess, most Jews are biblically illiterate. North American Jews are akin to North American Gentiles, in that most lack an even fundamental understanding of biblical teaching, either Old Testament or New!

Our mission statement is simple and to the point:

We boldly declare Y'shua as Messiah to the Jewish people; we urgently equip God's people to do the same.

The best way to bring the Gospel to someone Jewish is in the context of a personal relationship. Most Christians today know Jewish people but have remained silent on matters of faith. I speak in LCMS congregations most of the Sundays in a given year. Each time, I ask two questions:

1. How many here know someone Jewish? By a show of hands most congregants do.

2. How many have spoken of Y'shua with their Jewish friends in the past year? The average response: four people per service. Such silence has severe consequences—people perishing outside of Christ.

We see our work as a partnership with local congregations. We offer presentations to cultivate new relationships with Christians who might share our commitment to Jewish evangelism. Such presentations not only demonstrate the Jewish roots of the Christian faith but also serve as a means by which church members might invite their Jewish friends to learn more about the Christian faith. Our popular presentations include "Christ is the Passover," "The Gospel in the Feasts of Israel," and "The Fall Feasts of Israel." For those who would like a presentation in their church, we can be reached at 1-888-51-APPLE to schedule a speaker.

We also seek to work inside the structure of the LCMS, keeping Jewish missions before the leadership and bringing to conventions various resolutions that affirm the need and the urgency for including Jewish people in the mission of the church. The Apple of His Eye is a Recognized Service Organization of the LCMS Board for World Missions. This means that we maintain our Lutheran distinctives and that we report with transparency the struggles and victories of our mission work.

Our direct evangelism is done in various ways (see our Web site: www.aohems.org). We take to the streets in public places with our own homemade Gospel tracts called "broadsides." We wear shirts that identify us as part of the group and that invite people to interact with us over the Gospel. We go to football games, baseball games, hot air balloon races, concerts, parades, art shows, and Jewish gatherings. By asking a straightforward question, "What do you think of Y'shua?" we invite Jews and Gentiles alike to consider the Gospel message. We train others to do these things through our Jewish evangelism seminars and short-term mission training events.

We have established branches of our ministry with full-time missionaries. We have helped to start ministries in Los Angeles, Houston, St. Louis, New York City, and Moscow. We take on the front line mission work, and we train others. The fruit from those outreaches is shared with local churches. We have developed an international prayer initiative for Jewish missions worldwide. This "prayer consortium," as we call it, is accomplished through the Internet. We receive and share prayer requests and pass them along to over five thousand people.

One way we have established new contacts is through chat rooms on the Internet. We have entered Jewish, atheist, and other rooms with a simple question: "What do you think of Y'shua?" One Jewish student at Princeton shared his name and address with us; we forwarded it to another missionary organization working in that area. They made contact and after a series of personal visits, the person confessed Y'shua as his Messiah.

Once we have contacts, we follow up by sending messianic literature and inviting people to discuss the Bible and its message. Those who come to faith, we pass on to other congregations. Some new Jewish believers join traditional church congregations; others seek out messianic congregations where the biblical festivals are practiced and where Jewish culture is explicitly shared.

POSITIVE ATTITUDES IN PREPARATION FOR WITNESSING

Perhaps you have a Jewish friend. You may have thought, "I really can't tell that Jewish person about Jesus, because he is Jewish! I don't want to offend him." To share your faith with Jewish people (or anyone for that matter), here are some helpful principles:

Develop an Attitude of Willingness to Tell Others about Y'shua

Having a willing spirit is key. Many people have moved away from willingly, actively talking about their personal faith. It is easier to talk about the weather, sports, politics, or the economy. But on matters of personal faith, we tend to withdraw or to become uncomfortable. Perhaps we lack self-confidence. Maybe we lack knowledge of Scripture or feel inferior when dealing with spiritual things. But the Lord has called us to be witnesses, and He will equip us. Our actions and our words are important.

Pray That God Will Change Hearts

Pray that the Holy Spirit will unlock closed hearts. Hearts are not changed because of words or deeds, but because the Holy Spirit moves and touches the individual, initiating and maturing faith. The person who helped me come to faith in Christ prayed for me daily for nearly two years. His faithful prayer availed much. Praying for your Jewish friends who are not yet believers is a powerful action that God will bless.

I have heard stories and testimonies of loved ones who have prayed for spouses for 30 or 40 years before they finally acknowledged Y'shua as Messiah. Consistent prayer will bring consistent results in God's time. But we can never rush God in these matters of great spiritual importance. As you pray for your Jewish friend, pray that God will give you wisdom, discernment, and understanding as you take courage in speaking the things of God.

God has not shouldered us with the responsibility of convincing people that Y'shua's claims are true. Rather, God gives us the privilege of proclaiming His name to all. When we do, we know that the God of Abraham, Isaac, and Jacob changes people's hearts. We can rest on that promise and press ahead, gently sharing the hope that is in us and feeling free to express the Good News of our Savior.

Develop Sincere, Trusting Friendships with Nonbelievers

Often, we speak only to our friends about spiritual things. You don't need to know someone for years before you can speak of spiritual things, but you do need to build a friendship. Build a bridge of trust over which your information can travel, and you will have gone a long way toward initiating personal evangelistic dialogue.

Seek opportunities to involve yourself in the lives of people for whom you are praying and witnessing. Drop a card or note to your Jewish friend during a special festival. If there is a wedding or birth within his family, send a card or note to express your joy. If your Jewish friend is experiencing a sickness or death in the family, mourn and sorrow together with him.

These opportunities demonstrate the love that Y'shua demonstrated to us. We can laugh with those who laugh and weep with those who weep, showing people that we care and letting them know that we respect and love them as human beings.

Listen, Listen Some More, Keep on Listening—Then Speak

Rather than telling someone about your beliefs, ask about his or hers. Ask what your Jewish friend believes and does. Does he attend a synagogue in the neighborhood? Has she celebrated a Jewish holiday recently, or will she do so in the near future? If so, ask what that holiday means to your Jewish friend. Ask him which of the "movements" of Jewish people he identifies with or belongs to and why.

By knowing and understanding where a person's faith life is, we can then tailor our conversation to urge him to investigate further the things of God. I want to know first of all where a person is spiritually before I share anything with him about my spiritual life. I want to know if this person is religious or not, and if so, to what degree. I want to know what he thinks about the Bible, and what his attitudes are toward God, sin, atonement, and redemption.

I want to know what a Jewish person believes about the Messiah, if the Messiah is to be a person or an age, perhaps if she's lost hope in a personal Messiah. I want to know what his attitude is toward Y'shua. Does she believe that Y'shua lived at all? Was Y'shua a person in history? A prophet? A great teacher?

Become interested and acquainted with your Jewish friend's concerns. You might consider asking how he feels about Israel or intermarriage, or if he believes that unity is possible between Jewish people and Christians. If so, how could unity be accomplished? You might mention that many Jewish people today believe in Y'shua as Messiah. Ask your friend what he thinks of such a movement or what he thinks about the Bible or Y'shua.

Simply and Personally Share Your Own Faith

One of the most important things you can do in relating to anybody, including Jewish people, is to tell of what God has done for you. Your own personal testimony is very important. People may argue around interpretations of the Bible or theological perspectives, but they cannot argue about another individual's personal experience.

Perhaps you think your testimony is not exciting. But list the many things God has done for you, and I'm sure you will find several that give glory to God and that communicate to others. Simply demonstrate that God is personal, caring, and loving, and that He has made Himself real to you.

Consider Peter's simple, yet powerful, confession in Matthew 16:13–17:

> Now when Jesus [Y'shua] came into the district of Caesarea Philippi, He asked His disciples, "Who do people say that the Son of Man is?" And they said, "Some say John the Baptist, others say Elijah, and others Jeremiah or one of the prophets." He [Y'shua] said to them, "But who do you say that I am?" Simon Peter replied, "You are the Christ, the Son of the living God." And Jesus [Y'shua] answered him, "Blessed are you, Simon Bar-Jonah! For flesh and blood has not revealed this to you, but My Father who is in heaven."

Seek Many Different Opportunities to Speak of Y'shua

Jewish people today are open to talking about spiritual things, especially when they don't fear that someone is out to change them from being

Jewish to being something else. Develop an open relationship and an attitude of honest exchange; your evangelistic dialogue will yield good opportunities and good fruit.

When presenting the Gospel, don't give spiritual indigestion to the person. Don't overfeed him with too many Scripture passages and too much spiritual food for thought. Share a little Good News over several visits, rather than a lot in a few visits. This way, you will not wear out your welcome, and you will leave the person with one or two concrete thoughts to think about rather than a host of things to ponder.

You might invite your Jewish friend to a home Bible discussion group or to a service at your congregation. Sometimes churches in local communities have special speakers who talk about things of interest to Jewish people or about Jewish evangelism. When you see or hear of these events, invite your friend to the service with you so that he can hear and consider for himself what is said.

Base Personal Evangelistic Dialogue on the Bible

The Word of God is sharper than any two-edged sword. It's alive and active, and its words can change hearts. We cannot force anyone through coercion or pressure tactics to believe that Y'shua is Messiah. The Holy Spirit and the living Word of God alone can do that. Get to know your Bible. Practice using it as a workman uses a tool so that you can develop the skill of a master craftsman.

Before you open your Bible, ask permission of your friend to show him something there. As you open the Bible, make sure that you don't figuratively step behind some invisible pulpit and that you don't speak with a sermonic, preachy tone.

If you are in the home of your Jewish friend, consider using his Bible. The order of books within the Jewish Bible is different from the Bible you normally use, but the words are the same. Many Jewish homes today have a copy of the Hebrew Scriptures translated from the Masoretic text. Ask your friend to read aloud from his Bible, giving him the opportunity to see, speak, and read God's Word for himself. Don't forget to share Old Testament passages that point toward the Messiah.

I have heard it said many times that the Gospel is only in the New Testament. But our God is the same yesterday, today, and forever. The good news that He is seeking to redeem us is predicted in the Old and fulfilled in the New. So for those who have not yet accepted the New Testament as an authoritative text, as many of my people claim, you can point to God's promises in the Hebrew Bible (Old Testament) to redeem us from our sin. Look for yourself!

Behold, the LORD's hand is not shortened, that it cannot save, or His ear dull, that it cannot hear; but your iniquities have made a separation between you and your God, and your sins have hidden His face from you so that He does not hear. (Isaiah 59:1–2)

The word of the LORD came to me: "What do you mean by repeating this proverb concerning the land of Israel, 'The fathers have eaten sour grapes, and the children's teeth are set on edge'? As I live, declares the Lord GOD, this proverb shall no more be used by you in Israel. Behold, all souls are Mine; the soul of the father as well as the soul of the son is Mine: the soul who sins shall die." (Ezekiel 18:1–4)

And many of those who sleep in the dust of the earth shall awake, some to everlasting life, and some to shame and everlasting contempt. (Daniel 12:2; v. 1 in the Hebrew text)

We have all become like one who is unclean, and all our righteous deeds are like a polluted garment. We all fade like a leaf, and our iniquities, like the wind, take us away. (Isaiah 64:6)

And Aaron shall lay both his hands on the head of the live goat, and confess over it all the iniquities of the people of Israel, and all their trangressions, all their sins. And he shall put them on the head of the goat and send it away into the wilderness by the hand of a man who is in readiness. The goat shall bear all their iniquities on itself to a remote area, and he shall let the goat go free in the wilderness. (Leviticus 16:21–22. Because Leviticus 16 covers in great detail the extent to which the Lord sought to make atonement for the sins of the Hebrew people, it is helpful to outline the chapter for ease in presenting its basic principles.)

If any one of the house of Israel or of the strangers who sojourn among them eats any blood, I will set My face against that person who eats blood and will cut him off from his people. For the life of the flesh is in the blood, and I have given it for you on the altar to make atonement for your souls, for it is the blood that makes atonement by the life. (Leviticus 17:10–11)

Behold, the days are coming, declares the LORD, when I will make a new covenant with the house of Israel and the house of Judah, not like the covenant that I made with their fathers on the day when I took them by the hand to bring them out of the land of Egypt, My covenant that they broke, though I was their husband, declares the LORD. But this is the covenant that I will make with the house of Israel after those days, declares the LORD: I will put My law within them, and I will write it on their hearts. And I will be their God, and they shall be My people. And no longer shall each one teach his neighbor and each his brother, saying, 'Know the LORD,' for they shall all know Me, from the least of them to the greatest, declares the LORD. For I will forgive their iniquity, and I will remember their sin no more. (Jeremiah 31:31–34)

Surely He has borne our griefs and carried our sorrows; yet we esteemed Him stricken, smitten by God, and afflicted. But He was wounded for our transgressions; He was crushed for our iniquities; upon Him was the chastisement that brought us peace, and with His stripes we are healed. All we like sheep have gone astray; we have turned every one to his own way; and the LORD has laid on Him the iniquity of us all. (Isaiah 53:4–6)

We continue to develop a growing library of messianic resources that are freely accessible to our workers, the Christian community, and those who have an interest in learning more about Jewish people and evangelism. I have authored several books and numerous articles, including *Beginning from Jerusalem, Win-Some Witnessing 101, Disowned,* and *Jewish Roots.* I have written over seventy Gospel tracts with a wide-ranging subject matter, from sports to spiritual. We also use the New Testament with messianic references listed.

HAVE WE BEEN FAITHFUL?

Many outreach programs are judged to be effective or ineffective based solely on numbers. Perhaps the more relevant question is: have we been faithful? The parable of the sower and the soil reminds me that our work is to go out regardless of the responsiveness of the soil. Our attitude remains the same: we are to cast Gospel seed about. We are also to encourage Christians in their witness. We have made a good start since we began in 1996, but we have a long way to go. Jewish people and Gentiles have come to faith. For that we thank God! What we can see is growing awareness of Christians to reach out to seek our help.

I stand on God's Word in the confidence that what we do will be fruitful:

Therefore, my beloved brothers, be steadfast, immovable, always abounding in the work of the Lord, knowing that in the Lord your labor is not in vain. (1 Corinthians 15:58)

American Indian Outreach Ministry

Clark Gies
Executive Director of the Council for Lutheran American Indian
Ministry, Fairfax, South Dakota

Background

Native Americans were the first people to live in the Americas, and they developed distinctive and highly sophisticated cultures long before colonial expansion brought Europeans to the Western world. When Columbus discovered the "New World," he called the people he met "Indians," mistakenly thinking he had landed in the Indies.

Native Americans played a key role in helping the European settlers survive in the new world, but relations between the two groups soon deteriorated. Most Europeans treated Native Americans fairly, but others cheated them and took their land.

In an effort to live together peacefully, the Indians made many treaties only to discover again and again the land-hungry newcomers' word was not trustworthy or that the government had no control over the unscrupulous and greedy. In time, the U.S. government created reservations to protect Indian lands, but in many cases, even these reservations were taken from the Indian people.

The Native American population is growing, with one of the highest birthrates in the country. According to the 2000 census, there are more than 4.1 million identified American Indian people who are members of four hundred fifty separate tribes. Of these, 2.5 million registered as

American Indian only, and an additional 1.6 million registered as American Indian and another race. About half of the American Indians live on reservations and half in rural or urban areas off the reservations. American Indians live in all fifty states of our nation.

Native Americans are a people with a strong commitment to family and cultural identity. But as a people, they suffer from many problems, including an overwhelming sense of alienation. Instead of being culturally close, great differences tend to separate many tribes. Native Americans are a highly diverse people, with most tribes having their own languages, customs, and religious beliefs. Along with this separation among the tribes, many Native Americans feel isolated from the mainstream of modern life. Dropout rates from schools are extremely high, and unemployment runs as high as 80 to 90 percent.

Many Indians feel trapped between two cultures. The educational system into which they were forced often demeaned their cultural heritage without preparing them to function in the white culture. This alienation often creates despair, widespread alcoholism, and a suicide rate three times the national average.

Despite the alienation they feel, Indian people are deeply spiritual. Although their religious beliefs vary, they share a desire to live in harmony with nature. Many believe this harmony can be maintained through ceremonial rituals. The medicine man is usually the spiritual leader who has the responsibility to mediate between the spirit world and the community. Despite long-term exposure to the Gospel and considerable mission effort, many Indian people have never been effectively evangelized. It is estimated that less than 10 percent and perhaps as few as 3 percent are Christian and confess Jesus as Savior. The exploitation of American Indians and a strong desire of Indian people to maintain their own cultural identity have created a resistance to the Gospel. Many also have found it difficult to hear the Gospel message from the white man whose word in past years could not always be trusted. The memory of past injustices dies slowly, but the Good News of God's forgiveness must also be shared with Indian people. There is a great need to proclaim the Gospel among them.

The Lutheran Church—Missouri Synod (LCMS), through its districts, has placed missionaries in a number of reservation settings and communities as pastors, Directors of Christian Outreach, and certified lay workers.

Opportunities exist to send more missionaries to other reservations and Indian communities. There is a great need to train and prepare American Indian leaders as full-time church workers to be sent to their own people with the Good News of Jesus Christ. At American Indian Lutheran churches and missions, Indian leaders want to become better prepared to assume leadership responsibilities. In 1992, the Council for Lutheran American Indian Ministries (CLAIM) was established to serve the church in meeting these needs and responsibilities, with Dr. Bill Heinicke as its Executive Director.

CLAIM is led by an elected nine-member board of directors who also serve as Synod's Advisory Standing Committee for American Indian Ministries. American Indians make up a majority on this board. CLAIM is incorporated and has been granted tax exempt status (501[c][3]) by the IRS. A charter member of the Association of Lutheran Mission Agencies (ALMA), CLAIM is also a Recognized Service Organization (RSO) of the LCMS. From its beginning CLAIM has raised funds in support of its mission goals and also publishes a newsletter entitled *Proclaim*.

CLAIM does not sponsor direct ministries on Indian reservations or in Indian communities. These are sponsored by various districts of the LCMS. Rather, CLAIM's priorities are to recruit and train more Indian people as workers in ministry and leadership and to inform and encourage the people of the LCMS to greater involvement and support of mission work among Indian people. At the present time, Rev. Clark Gies serves as the Executive Director of CLAIM.

A Brief History of LCMS American Indian Ministry

In 1837, ten years prior to the formal organization of the LCMS in 1847, the Lutheran Leipzig mission of Leipzig, Germany, sent pastors and laypeople to the United States to establish missions among the American Indians. Edward R. Baierlein, Ottomar E. Cloeter, Fredrich A. Craemer, and Ernst Gustab Hermann Miessler were among those first sent by Wilhelm Loehe to Michigan near Saginaw Bay to begin mission work among the Chippewa Indians in that area. Baierlein erected a log cabin for his home and cleared some land, setting some aside as "God's acre," and named the place Bethany. In a remarkably short time, he had mastered the Chippewa language and had a book printed in the Chippewa language, which included portions of Luther's Small Catechism. In 1846, Craemer baptized the first Chippewa Indians as part of the Lutheran mission effort in Michigan. Most of those who had begun the mission remained and established the town of Frankenmuth, Michigan, and St. Lorenz Lutheran Church. After the breakup of the mission, Cloeter became an Indian missionary to Chippewa in Minnesota at Mille Lac, and then at Crow Wing.

Friedrich Wyneken, one of the founding fathers of the LCMS, also supported by Wilhelm Loehe's Lutheran Leipzig Society, served as an itinerant missionary among Native Americans in Indiana, Ohio, and Michigan.

Moritz Braueninger, also sent by Wilhelm Loehe's society, served as a missionary to the Crow Indians near Fort Sarpy, Montana, in 1858. In 1859, along with two others, he erected an Indian mission station on the Powder River in eastern Oregon. According to reports, he was shot by one of a group of Indians on July 22, 1860.

During the 1870s, Iowa Lutherans attempted mission work with the Crow and Cheyenne tribes, but their efforts did not start any missions. In 1898, the Stockbridge-Munsee tribe in Wisconsin appealed to the LCMS for a pastor, and Rev. Nichol responded and established Immanuel Lutheran Church. Immanuel is the oldest American Indian congregation in the LCMS. Immanuel had a parochial school for over fifty years, until it was closed in 1958.

From the turn of the century until the mid-1960s, there was little formal, organized mission work among American Indians by the LCMS. If a congregation or a pastor near an Indian reservation or Indian settlement took interest in doing mission work in their area, some activity would happen until the pastor accepted a call to another location, but there was no established, ongoing mission activity on the part of districts of the LCMS or the Synod itself until 1964.

Beginning in 1964, when the Rev. Walter Weber was called by the LCMS to be its National Indian Ministry Consultant, the Synod and its districts began specific outreach activities to the American Indian population. Rev. Weber, living first in Pierre, South Dakota, and later in Sioux Falls, consulted with many Indian tribes and LCMS districts about the possibility of beginning Indian ministry in their areas. As a result of Rev. Weber's efforts, in 1966 the Rev. Clark Gies was called to be Reservation Missionary and Coordinator of Religious Activities on the Pine Ridge Reservation in South Dakota, and in 1968 the South Dakota District called Larry Belitz to be a teacher-evangelist on the reservation. In 1969, the Rocky Mountain District opened a mission on the Navajo Reservation at Navajo, New Mexico, and called the Rev. Don Bren as a missionary. Three years later, in 1972, Wiley Scott, a Cree Indian, and his wife, Caryn, began the LIGHT House, a ministry to students at the Haskell All Nations Indian University in Lawrence, Kansas. They opened their home as a Lutheran student center at the university. In 1974, the Northwest District called the Rev. Don Johnson, a Makah Indian, to begin a mission at Neah Bay, Washington, on his home reservation. In 1977, the Wyoming District called Rev. Bren from the Navajo Reservation to begin mission work on the Wind River Reservation at Fort Washakie. In 1982, the Rev. Dennis Bauer was called by the Montana District to begin work on the Northern Cheyenne Reservation near Lame Deer, Montana. Dan Jacobs began work as a vicar on the Crow Reservation in 1984 and was called by the district in 1986 to return to the reservation as missionary-pastor at Crow Agency, Montana. In 1991, after several years of not having a resident pastor, Steve Hyvonen began a two-year vicarage at Immanuel Mohican Church near Gresham, Wisconsin, and returned in 1994 as missionary-pastor at Immanuel Mohican. Three new LCMS Indian missions began in 1993: Rev. Richard Latterner, an Ojibwa Indian, was called by the Minnesota North District to begin mission on the Leech Lake and White Earth Reservations in Minnesota; Rev. Ricky Jacob was called by the Nebraska District to begin mission work on the Winnebago Indian Reservation at Winnebago, Nebraska; and Rev. Robert Utecht was called by the South Dakota District to do Indian Ministry in the Rosebud Reservation in South Dakota. In 1998, Rev. Jeff Warner was called by the Nebraska District to begin ministry on the Omaha Reservation in Nebraska, and Sheila Peterson, a Director of Christian Outreach, was called by the Minnesota North District to be a missionary-evangelist on the Fond du Lac Reservation in Minnesota. In 2001, Rev. Bruce Alberts began outreach to the Cherokee Nation at Tallequah, Oklahoma, and Steve Watkins was commissioned as a lay minister by the Pacific Southwest District on the Navajo Reservation in Arizona.

CURRENT AMERICAN INDIAN MINISTRIES AND MISSION OUTREACH BY THE LCMS

Immanuel Mohican Church, Wisconsin

It was in 1899 that the LCMS began to provide services to a group of Stockbridge-Munsee Christian people located on a reservation near

Shawano, Wisconsin, in a community called Red Springs. The Stock-bridge-Munsee group, also referred to as Mohicans, came to Wisconsin about forty years earlier from Massachusetts by way of New York. Origi-nally converted to Christianity by Congregational missionaries, most of the group became Presbyterians during their fifty-year sojourn in New York. They requested the services of the LCMS when their pastor of many years passed away and the Presbyterian Church was unable to provide a successor. At the same time, German immigrants were coming into the area as farmers and the Stockbridge-Munsee group asked one of their pastors to serve them.

After not having called a pastor since 1958, Immanuel Mohican, located on the Stockbridge-Munsee Reservation in Northern Wisconsin, through the North Wisconsin District, called its former vicar, Rev. Steve Hyvonen as its pastor in 1994. Blessed by the Holy Spirit, under the leadership of Pastor Hyvonen, and now Pastor Tim Lankin, who vicared at Immanuel from 1993 to 1994 and later succeeded Pastor Hyvonen as Immanuel's pastor, the congregation was energized in the following ways: it increased its evange-lism outreach, held Bible studies, renovated its building, and gathered for weekly worship. Further, a greater awareness of the needs of the people led new members to join, spurred an increase in worship attendance, and gen-erated a plan to continue evangelism among American Indians in North Wisconsin. There is a desire on the part of the people to have the Gospel preached regularly, to celebrate the Lord's Supper frequently, and to expand God's kingdom of grace in North Wisconsin.

Pine Ridge Sioux Reservation, South Dakota

In 1966, the Rev. Clark Gies was called by the South Dakota District of the LCMS as Reservation Missionary and Coordinator of Religious Activ-ities on the Pine Ridge Reservation in southwestern South Dakota. He established the Pine Ridge Lutheran Fellowship in the town of Pine Ridge and held worship services and taught the Christian faith in Sunday School, midweek school, and Bible studies. As a means of establishing relationships and finding opportunities for Christian witness, Rev. Gies served in several capacities throughout the community: counselor at the Oglala Community School in Pine Ridge, counselor for the Neighbor-hood Youth Corps, counselor at the Pine Ridge Moccasin Factory, board member of the Pine Ridge Development Corporation, member of the

Pine Ridge Reservation Education Committee, and member of the Pine Ridge Boy Scouts Committee.

Two years after Rev. Gies arrived, the South Dakota District also called Larry Belitz as teacher-evangelist on the Pine Ridge Reservation. Since his arrival in 1968, Larry has had portions of the New Testament translated into the Lakota language and created witnessing tracts that present a Christian witness built on the four virtues (wisdom, generosity, bravery, and endurance) of the Lakota nation. These materials are very popular and are distributed at wakes, powwows, and memorial "giveaways." Because Larry is an adopted Sioux, in the way that a Lakota family honors and makes someone a family member, he has many occasions to attend events not open to the general public.

For the past thirty-seven years, Larry has worked on traditional Lakota crafts. He has learned how to make many traditional crafts in the ways they were made over 100 years ago. Much of the knowledge of traditional craft techniques has long been forgotten on the reservation and Larry teaches those interested in learning about their Lakota heritage. Larry has also helped produce five movies on Native Americans, including *Dances with Wolves*. His understanding of, and ability to produce, traditional Native American craft work also helps enable Larry to present the message of salvation through Jesus Christ in a way that it is heard. Since much of Larry's ministry is conducted in personal, one-on-one relationships, he is able to present the Gospel in a way that is acceptable and effective.

Bible studies, led by Pastor Bob Utecht, are held every two weeks on the reservation in the village of Porcupine. At the same time, Sunday School with lessons and crafts is held for the children. Vacation Bible School is also held at several locations on the reservation every summer. As is traditional in the Lakota culture, the Bible studies, Sunday School, and VBS include a mealtime.

Shepherd of the Valley Lutheran Church on the Navajo Reservation

Home to about two hundred fifty thousand people, the Navajo Reservation is the largest single reservation in the United States. The reservation covers territory in the states of Arizona, New Mexico, and Utah. In 1969, the Rocky Mountain District of the LCMS called the Rev. Don Bren to establish a mission station in the New Mexico portion of the reservation in the town of Navajo, New Mexico, about twenty-five miles northeast of

Window Rock, Arizona, where the Navajo Tribal Headquarters is located. Since 1988, the Rev. Steve Greene has served Shepherd of the Valley Lutheran Church and additional outlying locations named Sawmill, White Clay, Two-Grey Hills, Window Rock, Shiprock, and Sheep Springs.

There is much human resistance to the Christian faith on the reservation. Many traditional people are greatly opposed to Christ, and Navajo Christians know persecution firsthand. Yet Pastor Greene reaches out into the broader areas of the reservation with home-based worship and instruction in the Christian faith. Pastor Greene is also involved with local drug abuse prevention and recovery, as well as self-help programs at Navajo. Outreach through parenting classes, a lending library of Christian books and videos, and women's Bible study groups also are ways of establishing relationships and sharing the Good News.

Louise Lee, a Navajo Indian and a member of Shepherd of the Valley Lutheran Congregation, is a commissioned full-time parish worker and assistant to Pastor Greene.

LIGHT (Lutheran Indians Gathering and Helping Together) at Haskell Indian Nations University in Lawrence, Kansas

Haskell LIGHT began in 1972 as a Lutheran ministry to the students, faculty, and staff of Haskell Indian Nations University (then an Indian Junior College) in Lawrence, Kansas. Wiley and Caryn Scott initiated a campus ministry with the help of Immanuel Lutheran Church in Lawrence. Wiley, a Cree Indian Lutheran and graduate of Haskell, and his wife, Caryn, recognized the need for a Lutheran ministry at Haskell and began gathering students together for fellowship and study.

Haskell Indian Nations University has an enrollment of about one thousand American Indian students from many tribes and reservations throughout the United States. Just across the street from the Haskell campus is the LIGHT House where students can find a place to study, socialize, receive tutoring, opportunity for Bible study, and receive spiritual and emotional support. The LIGHT House provides Haskell students, many very far from home, a needed safe place where they can find an open Christian welcome, love, encouragement, and guidance. Homemade blankets from individuals and church groups (primarily the societies of the Lutheran Women's Missionary League) are always appreciated by the students, many of whom have little more than the clothes on their backs when they arrive on campus. Bibles and devotional materials are always provided free of charge. Free tickets to theater and sporting events are also often provided to students. In all of these activities, sharing the Word with the students is the first priority.

In 1985, the LIGHT House employed its first director. Since that time, Wiley and Caryn have continued to fill the vacancies between directors, and presently are again interim directors.

Makah Lutheran Church, Makah Reservation, Neah Bay, Washington

In 1974, the Northwest District of the LCMS called candidate Rev. Don Johnson to begin a ministry among the Makah Indian people at Neah Bay, Washington. The Makah Reservation covers twenty-eight square miles of land and is home to about two thousand Makah Indians. Pastor Johnson, himself a Makah Indian, established the Makah Lutheran Church and served as its pastor until 1993, at which time he accepted the position of Missions Director for Lutheran Association of Missionaries and Pilots. Rev. Don Smith, who vicared at Neah Bay in 1991, returned there as the new pastor of Makah Lutheran Church, being installed on July 18, 1993.

Presently, the Rev. Dale Heinlein serves as pastor of Makah Lutheran Church. Since coming to Neah Bay in 2000, Pastor Heinlein has emphasized the importance of speaking to the Makah people in their native language. His overall goal is to assist and enable people to worship in their unique Makah way.

Both Dale and his wife, Dianne, studied the Makah language at the local college. Those who worship at Makah Lutheran Church and local children who attend church events are taught songs and the Lord's Prayer in Makah.

In 2002, Dale and Dianne opened a Christian Youth Center, which is staffed by Dianne. Two afternoons a week the center is open to middle school students, and two evenings a week it is open to high school students. The sessions are a combination of discussions, Bible studies, cooking projects, and free time to use the center's pool tables, foosball table, video games, karaoke machine, board games, keyboard, and television.

Dale is also mentoring David Sternbeck, a Makah man, who is completing his first year of pastoral study in the Ethnic and Immigrant Institute of Theology through Concordia Seminary in St. Louis. Upon completion of his studies, David will become a pastor at Makah Lutheran Church. Reaching out from Neah Bay, Dale and Dave are also ministering to people on other nearby reservations in Washington.

Wind River Lutheran Mission, Fort Washakie, Wyoming, on the Wind River Reservation, Wyoming

Wind River Reservation in Wyoming encompasses around 3,500 square miles and is home to two Indian tribes: the Eastern Band of the Shoshone and the Northern Band of the Arapahoe. Between the two tribes there are approximately seven thousand men, women, and children (two thousand Shoshone and five thousand Arapahoe). The tribes have jointly owned tribal lands and have a Joint Business Council.

In 1977, the Wyoming District of the LCMS called the Rev. Don Bren, who was serving on the Navajo Reservation in New Mexico, to begin work on the Wind River Reservation. Work first was begun at Fort Washakie among the Shoshone people, and then at Crowheart, also among the Shoshone.

After spending his vicarage year on Wind River Reservation in 1986, Rev. Don Browne, a Crow Indian, was called back to Fort Washakie on the Wind River and the church commissioned him to serve as a missionary on the reservation in September of 1987, where he served until 1997. While serving at Fort Washakie, Pastor Browne established the Wind River Lutheran Mission.

Rev. Vern Boehlke, having just retired from the pastoral ministry, accepted a call to minister among the Shoshone people of the Wind River Reservation in Wyoming in a semiretired capacity in 1998. Under his guidance, two vicars, Len Astrowski in 2002 and Don Nemec in 2003, have also served the people of the Wind River Reservation at Fort Washakie and Crowheart. At the present time, Rev. Boehlke has again returned to serve as interim pastor.

The church gathers regularly for Sunday worship, Sunday School, and Bible classes. They also hold VBS, summer outings, youth and adult confirmation classes, and monthly clothing giveaways, which provide an opportunity for witnessing through handing out tracts and inspirational booklets. All of these activities are means by which ministry is carried out so that the people of Wind River might know more about their Savior.

Circle of Life Lutheran Church, Muddy Cluster, Montana, on the Northern Cheyenne Reservation in Montana

Back in 1876, the Sioux and Cheyenne Indians joined together at the Little Big Horn River in southeastern Montana to defeat Gen. George Custer and the Seventh Calvary. About twenty miles east of this historic site is the Northern Cheyenne Reservation, home to about four thousand Cheyenne Indian people. It is this reservation where Circle of Life Lutheran Church is located in the small community of Muddy Cluster.

In 1982, the Rev. Dennis Bauer was called by the Montana District of the LCMS to begin a ministry on the Northern Cheyenne Reservation. Pastor Bauer discovered that almost all traditional religious ceremonies of the Northern Cheyenne people are held in a circular format or structure; consequently, the circular design was incorporated into the facility used by Circle of Life Lutheran Church for the congregation's many activities, including Christian worship and fellowship. The facility is also used as a center for community activity and life in Muddy Cluster.

Congregational activities include the Sunday worship, adult and children's Sunday School, an active program for senior and junior youth, and a Christian support group. In all of these, Pastor Bauer seeks to develop experiences using Northern Cheyenne cultural traditions. Pastor Bauer also leads spiritual retreats to Bear Butte, a mountain in South Dakota near the Black Hills, which the traditional Cheyenne people consider consecrated, and also has camping programs for the youth of the reservation.

The latest venture undertaken by Pastor Bauer, along with lay involvement from Carmel Lutheran Church, Carmel, Indiana, is the development of a youth camp. The purpose of the camp is to create a place to work with kids holistically, including both traditional native values and faith. A number of the cabins for the camp have been constructed, and work on two others is underway.

Crow Indian Reservation, Montana

In 1984, Vicar Dan Jacobs was assigned by the Montana District of the LCMS to begin Lutheran mission work on the Crow Indian Reservation. In 1986, Pastor Jacobs was called back to the reservation by the district. Since then, Pastor Jacobs' activities include Sunday worship services, several regular Bible study sessions, after-school programs for school children, and many visits within the Crow reservation community.

Pastor Jacobs also sponsors a booth at the annual "Crow Fair," one of the country's largest gatherings of American Indian people. The booth at the Crow Fair is an important part of the Lutheran presence on the reservation. At the fair, Bibles and other Christian literature are given out. Bible studies on the resurrection, on suffering, and on being a Christian are handed out. Vacation Bible School is also held at the booth.

Through involvement in the communities as neighbors, at powwows, in teaching and studying at the reservation college, the Rev. Jacobs and his family have built lasting relationships with the Crow people. Learning the Crow language and culture has also been very helpful in the ministry. Pastor Jacobs has developed the "Crow Language Alphabet Book," which applies Scripture through various illustrations. Using Crow stories that help teach the Ten Commandments, and other stories that serve as parables or analogies of redemption, is also very beneficial to the ministry. Sharing food and helping families in need, and translating Bible stories into Crow, all have helped in sharing the Gospel in meaningful ways.

Pastor Jacobs also reaches out to people in the community of Lodge Grass on the Crow reservation, at Under the Shadow of His Wings Lutheran Church, and to other reservation areas in Montana.

All Nations Lutheran Mission, Leech Lake Reservation, Minnesota

In 1993, a group of five pastors expressed concern and interest that no Lutheran church was active and working among the Ojibwa Indian people of the White Earth and the Leech Lake Indian Reservations in north-central Minnesota. These pastors expressed the concern to Rev. Paul Biegner, Executive Director of Missions of the Minnesota North District of the LCMS. As a result, Richard Latterner, an Ojibwa Indian, who had just completed his required courses at Concordia Seminary, Fort Wayne, Indiana, was assigned to do his vicarage work on both reservations. After completing his vicarage, Pastor Latterner was then called as pastor-missionary to the Ojibwa people of the Leech Lake Reservation, where he served until December 1997. While serving on the reservation, which has a population of ten thousand, Pastor Latterner developed a series of Bible study lessons that are directly related to the needs and situations of Indian people. He also was instrumental in organizing an Indian

Lutheran congregation on the Leech Lake Reservation at Cass Lake, Minnesota, called All Nations Lutheran Mission.

The Rev. Mark Peske, who served his vicarage under Pastor Latterner at Cass Lake in 1995 and 1996, has served as missionary-pastor on the Leech Lake Reservation since 1997. Pastor Peske's ministry focus has much to do with building relationships and continuing to learn about the local Native American culture. His outreach has included harvesting wild rice with community members, teaching an optional religious instruction class at the local school, leading Bible study at the local jail, guiding people through the Fifth Step of Alcoholics Anonymous at a treatment center, leading youth on camping trips, and a very concentrated ministry to Native American men.

Jesus Our Savior Lutheran Church, Winnebago, Nebraska, Winnebago Reservation

The Winnebago Reservation in northeast Nebraska is home to about 1,650 tribal members. In a formal resolution to the Nebraska District of the LCMS, the Winnebago Tribal Council, Winnebago, Nebraska, specifically requested the LCMS to place a youth counselor on the Winnebago Reservation. Just as importantly, the tribe stated that the person requested is invited to share the Christian faith and engage in mission and ministry with the Winnebago people. In July of 1993, the Rev. Ricky Jacob was called by the Nebraska District and began full-time work on the reservation.

Pastor Jacob, after making the effort to learn and understand the language and culture by taking courses at the local tribal college and also taking courses in the area of counseling, is using the knowledge and wisdom he gained to faithfully preach and teach the Gospel message in ways and means that are not offensive to the hearers. By 1994, Pastor Jacob had started a worship group that calls itself Jesus Our Savior Lutheran Church. As opportunities arise, he is able to share his faith and spiritual beliefs with the people of Winnebago. His office is also a Christian resource center with books and videos for people of all ages. Pastor Jacob also writes a column for the local newspaper and hosts volunteer mission teams that come to the reservation to provide services of various kinds to the people of the reservation.

Jesus Our Savior Lutheran Preschool, with Jana Inglehart as its teacher, has completed seven years of reaching the children of the Winnebago Tribe with the saving message of the Gospel. In addition, some "graduates" of the preschool have gone on to attend Zion Lutheran School in Bancroft, Nebraska, which is twenty-eight miles from Winnebago. Recently, the Winnebago Tribal Council has asked Jesus Our Savior Lutheran Preschool to begin a Lutheran elementary school on the reservation, and initial planning is underway to fulfill the request.

Rosebud Indian Lutheran Church, Rosebud, South Dakota, on the Rosebud Reservation in South Dakota

In October 1993, Rev. Bob Utecht was commissioned by the South Dakota District of the LCMS as a Missionary-At-Large on the Rosebud Sioux Reservation in South Dakota. The reservation is home to about thirteen thousand Sioux people. As part of his outreach, Pastor Utecht regularly broadcast daily and Sunday devotional programs over the local Native American radio station. He also conducted a midweek Bible study for children in the community of Grass Mountain, a Bible study for the people in the Lower Cut Meat community, and Sunday worship and fellowship in the town of Rosebud.

In 1996, Rev. Utecht's son, Andrew, vicared on the Rosebud Reservation and was called by the South Dakota District as Missionary-at-Large, and he eventually took over the mission upon Pastor Bob Utecht's retirement. He now pastors Rosebud Indian Lutheran Church in Rosebud and also a small congregation fifteen miles away in the village of Parmalee, called Lord's Warrior's Lutheran Church.

Using a trailer whose sides fold down to become a stage, Pastor Bob Utecht and Pastor Andrew Utecht use puppets and magic to present the biblical stories of creation, man's fall into sin, the birth of the Savior, Jesus' crucifixion, the resurrection, and second coming. Following the Christian lessons, there is always a lunch or refreshments served. Perhaps the most rewarding time each week is the midweek Bible school for kids. There, the students are taught the basics of the Christian faith, using Bible stories, crafts, videos, puppets, and magic tricks.

Each summer, free ice water is passed out at the Rosebud Fair and Powwow. This presents an opportunity to establish relationships, to witness, and to be a positive influence in the community.

Fond du Lac Reservation, Minnesota

Our Redeemer Lutheran Church in Cloquet, Minnesota, is directly adjacent to the Fond du Lac Ojibwa Indian Reservation in northeastern Minnesota. Led by Pastor John Lehenbauer, in the early 1990s, the congregation began an active outreach to the American Indian community. Marilu Johnson, an Ojibwa member of the congregation, also has worked as an American Indian Outreach worker among her people. Elders and Indian members of the congregation conducted Bible studies with students at the local community college, sponsored a weekly jail ministry, and conducted individual Bible studies with a number of Indian women. The congregation also conducted a summer VBS program in which several Indian children were enrolled. Following the VBS, Pastor Lehenbauer began a home Bible study group with the children's parents.

In 1998, the Minnesota North District of the LCMS called Sheila Peterson to serve as family counselor-evangelist on the Fond du Lac Reservation. Sheila, a graduate of the Oswald Hoffman School of Outreach at Concordia University in St. Paul, Minnesota, is a Director of Christian Outreach. Her office is located in Our Redeemer Lutheran Church in Cloquet, where she and her husband Bob are members. As part of her evangelism effort, she has begun to learn both the Ojibwa language and culture. As a result of the relationships formed, many through VBS, she has distributed quilts, health kits, and school kits to many families. A room in the community center built by the tribe was offered as a place to conduct VBS and also a year-round weekly children's program. Sheila not only ensures that the children have a positive experience but also takes extra effort to give them opportunities to learn about their own Native American culture, learning how to harvest wild rice and make birch baskets as she shares with them the Good News.

Omaha Reservation, Nebraska

In October of 1997, Rev. Jeff Warner was installed by the Nebraska District of the LCMS as missionary-counselor to the Indian people of Nebraska's Omaha Indian Reservation at Macy, Nebraska. Rev. Warner works with residents of the local nursing home, the drug-alcohol treatment center, the center for abused children, and among the prisoners in the tribal jail. He also conducts worship services at the nursing home. Pastor Warner makes listening to the people a priority. Hearing of the life experience of the people, with almost every story tragic at some level, he is able to offer spiritual strength as he shares God's Good News of redemption in Jesus Christ. Under the Lord's blessing, Pastor Warner has established the My People Lutheran Outreach Church.

Cherokee Nation, Oklahoma

The Rev. Bruce Alberts, pastor of First Lutheran Church in Tallequah, Oklahoma, ministers to the Cherokee of Oklahoma. The Cherokee of Oklahoma consider Christianity to be a major part of their heritage. In fact, the Cherokee of Oklahoma feel that they are the ones who brought Christianity to Oklahoma. Therefore Pastor Alberts feels that as a missionary to the Cherokee, his calling is to bring to the Cherokee more of what they already have: more Good News of salvation through Jesus Christ. Using large community events in their church to reach the general public, First Lutheran has been blessed to have several Native Americans respond and attend services.

The Challenge

Knowing that relations with Native Americans are rooted in a bitter past, pastors, missionaries, directors of Christian outreach, lay ministers, and others involved in Indian ministry strive to build trust and to make the churches culturally relevant. These workers and their families involved in Indian ministry put much energy into their mission. This is a challenging ministry, but there are reasons to hope. Building effective relationships that will allow for the sharing of the Gospel takes time, great patience, a long-term commitment to the ministry, and a genuine love that flows out of Christ's love for us.

As CLAIM pursues its primary purpose of identifying, training, and equipping more American Indian people for leadership roles in ministry; supporting the pastors, missionaries, and laypeople working on the reservations in establishing ministries among Native American people, the partnership of the people of the LCMS is vital.

We are so thankful for the interest and support shown for Indian ministry through prayers and financial gifts which allow the missionaries to continue their work and support Native American students who desire to become Christian spiritual leaders among their people.

Outreach Ministry
to African Americans

Roosevelt Gray
Director of Missions, Michigan District of The Lutheran
Church—Missouri Synod, Ann Arbor, Michigan

Gospel Centered, Mission Focused,
and People Sensitive

The objectives and goals of outreach ministry in the African American context are not unlike outreach ministry among other ethnic groups. But specifically, when one identifies the reaching congregations in the Black community, one sees a ministry and mission that is threefold in purpose and scope: Its center is the Gospel, its focus is mission, and it is sensitive to people at its core. Outreach without taking these components into account is often ineffective at best. This model is the Great Commission in a nutshell: Gospel-centered, mission-focused, and people-sensitive. It is a wholistic approach to serving people and making disciples as Christ has commanded His church in Matthew 28:16–20, and it is truly a model that our Savior used Himself.

Christ as the Model

Christ used this model as He sought to serve. Consider a few Scripture texts that demonstrate how Christ saw the Gospel impacting the lives of people where they lived every day. In the Matthew 9:35–38 narrative, Christ sought the people where they lived and in their everyday struggles.

31

He preached the Good News of the kingdom. He healed their diseases and sicknesses. He had compassion on them. He saw their need to be connected to God and asked the disciples to pray to the God of the harvest to send more workers in the harvest field. But He did not leave it at that; Christ then sent the disciples out to do the same, to model this mission mandate for the kingdom of God. This was three pronged and wholistic in its goals and objectives: Gospel, mission, people.

Notice Christ's announcement and approach in Luke 4:18–19. He is quoting from the Old Testament prophet Isaiah (Isaiah 61:1–2), as Christ is fulfilling the Old Testament prophecy and ushering in the messianic age. Here we see a Gospel-centered, mission-focused, and people-sensitive approach to mission and ministry outreach.

The Rev. Dr. John Nunes, in his book *Voices from the City*, interviewed and quoted many African American and urban pastors who are still serving in the heart of the city. As each of them spoke, he gave credence to the need of this wholistic approach to outreach ministry; it is Gospel-centered, mission-focused, and people-sensitive. These pastors spoke of the need to stay Gospel-centered; that is to be incarnational, correctly dividing Law and Gospel as you deal with the brokenness of sinful lives and providing a Gospel-centered means of grace in the Word and Sacraments as effective freedom from the poverty of sin and its consequences.

You notice how this approach has a scriptural foundation, a Lutheran foundation based on grace, faith, and the Scriptures. Christ understood that God cared about people, not buildings and traditions. He engaged the religious ruling authorities constantly in their need to be servants of the spirit of the law and not the letter of the law. He pleaded with them to proclaim God's broad wholistic counsel of the forgiveness of sins, spiritual healing, physically and socially living as a disciple of the God who loved the world so much that He gave His all, His Son as an atoning sacrifice for all people (John 3:16).

The goal of this chapter is to help Christians in general and Lutherans in particular to see outreach ministry from a wholistic approach as stated earlier.

Lutheran Christian Theology and Wholistic Outreach

Lutheran theology is wholistic theology. Lutheran theology centers its ministry and mission from the Holy Scriptures, the source and norm of all

Christian doctrine. The Lutheran Confessions, therefore, state: "We believe, teach, and confess that the sole rule and standard according to which all dogmas together with all teachers should be estimated and judged are the prophetic and apostolic Scriptures of the Old and New Testament alone" (*Triglot*, 777).

As Lutheran Christians, we understand that the very foundation of the church is built on the confession of Peter:

> Now when Jesus came into the district of Caesarea Philippi, He asked His disciples, "Who do people say that the Son of Man is?" And they said, "Some say John the Baptist, others say Elijah, and others Jeremiah or one of the prophets." He said to them, "But who do you say that I am?" Simon Peter replied, "You are the Christ, the Son of the living God." (Matthew 16:13–16)

This is the fundamental question and answer of the church to the world. Jesus is the Christ, the Son of the living God. And in this Christ, God has chosen to reveal Himself to the world. In this Christ, God has confronted humanity's mortality and provided a means for immortality. In this Christ, God has restored paradise. In this Christ, God has restored His relationship with humanity, both spiritually and physically through the means of grace: the Word and Sacraments.

MODELS OF OUTREACH IN THE AFRICAN AMERICAN CONTEXT

Mission and ministry in any context have at their core the Gospel, missions, and people; yet we do not reach out to people in a vacuum. Outreach is done among people who have real needs; yes, a need to be converted from sin, Satan, death, and hell, but also the need to exist as divinely created and re-created images of God. People are not sent directly to heaven when they are converted to faith in Christ. Christians are left here on earth to be witnesses (Acts 1:8) of the wonderful work of the Gospel. People have specific needs (Acts 6:1–7) as they proclaim and live out that message every day as a witness to Christ. God has provided for those needs not only through the society in which they live (Psalm 24:1) but also through the lives of His church, the people of God.

Therefore it is very important to proclaim the Gospel in a way that is sensitive to the context of the people to whom we are witnessing. The message of the Gospel never changes, but the venue, the community, the culture in which it is proclaimed is almost always different. One community could benefit from a Christian day school, another from a Head Start program or Charter School, which are government sponsored. One community could benefit from senior citizen housing, another from providing resources for growing families. One community could benefit from a dynamic youth program, another from serving single moms. A community could have as its basic need crime prevention, another serving delinquent youth. One community may have a need to serve indigent homeless people, another decent affordable housing.

Some Effective Models That Are Observable in the African American Context

Senior Citizen Care is a mission and ministry serving its community by providing a space for senior citizens to meet in partnership with AARP and other community agencies. These agencies provide medical and prescription screening and advice to senior citizens. The congregation's facility becomes a place where senior citizens and the helping agencies can meet together in a Christian safe environment. The pastor has opportunity to greet people in this setting, listen and provide spiritual conversation when needed. Oftentimes these agencies will gladly give the pastor an opportunity to share with the seniors the history of the congregation's mission to the community and an opening prayer for the participants.

For individuals on the other end of the life spectrum, groups have run Head Start programs from the basement of churches from the very inception of the program. Many of these families live in direct shadow of the steeple and cross of the church. Though Head Start is a government operated program, the pastor and people of the church have many opportunities to volunteer and interact with families and children. Workers and children are often members of the congregation itself because the need of the community is not foreign to the needs of the people in the pew.

The Charter School program, though not in every state of the United States, has become a growing education delivery system in many states. Congregations who no longer can provide a Christian day school but have a large education facility are now leasing their facilities to these privately owned government subsidized schools. Many of these schools have Lutheran Christian teachers and principals teaching and interacting with these young lives at such an impressionable age. Some congregations have provided after-school programs and catechism instruction as additional coordinated efforts to meet the needs of children.

The Senior Citizen Housing program is a program congregations are providing with the partnership and assistance of Lutheran Homes of America, the U.S. Department of Housing (HUD), and Presbyterian Village. This partnership helps senior citizens of low income with affordable living accommodation in their retirement years. These seniors often worship and become members of the congregations providing the housing assistance.

The Community Development Cooperation is used by a variety of congregations to enhance the life of the community by utilizing federal, state, and local resources to revitalize declining communities. This 501(c)(3) nonprofit cooperation involves collaboration with other Christian organizations and service groups in the community.

The Indigent Ministry program serves those whose lives have been affected by drugs, crime, and prison. This program provides a place of worship, counseling, and a process for rehabilitation.

The Clothing and Food Bank program is a ministry providing affordable clothing and food for people who are in need for such assistance. This program meets the most basic needs of the community—food and clothing.

The Work of Mission Societies

Benton Harbor Lutheran Outreach Ministry in Michigan is an outreach ministry creating partnerships and connecting with the churches, as well as city and other agencies, to serve people. This program, which partnered with Habitat for Humanity to help gather volunteers to build affordable homes for people in the Benton Harbor community, also provides other tangible resources to people in the community.

Lutheran City Ministry is a mission society that plants new missions and partners with existing congregations to serve communities. There are various after-school programs, youth programs, and singing programs connecting people to the church.

The ministries and service opportunities mentioned above are not really new ventures of serving people in the communities where they live. These are simple ways of identifying with the felt needs of a particular community as the church goes about the work of the Great Commission, proclaiming the saving Gospel of Jesus Christ. The church has always been about serving, sharing, and saving communities (Acts 2:42–47).

Lutherans have always been in ministry to the whole person. Many of these ministry opportunities have been done by separate agencies serving on behalf of local congregations. The Lutheran Church has the largest social service agencies in the United States and around the world, which is testament to the thought that God is the God of the whole person. But perhaps now is the time for local congregations to become more personally involved in such service so they may have a greater opportunity to proclaim the Gospel to those who are so desperately in need of the gift of God's love and grace. God's love and grace found only in His Son, Jesus Christ, is the only motivation for serving people, no matter what the mission or ministry opportunities are in a particular community. Outreach ministry is ultimately about connecting and reconciling people to our gracious God, who gave us the greatest servant of all, His Son, our Savior. If this is not our motivation, then these mission and ministry opportunities are nothing more than busy social activities: but when done under the love for the Gospel, they become a means whereby God provides His love and grace to the world.

RESOURCES

Some books to enhance your understanding in this area include:

Voices from the City, by John Nunes (Concordia)

Rev. Nunes listens and allows the voices of those serving in the urban context to come forth and bring to life the challenges and joys of serving in an urban arena. *Voices from the City* is a must read for those who would remain in the heart of urban communities serving people. It is a book of pungent perspectives and inescapable realities for anyone involved in ministry, period. It gives voice to the clarity of sound scriptural Lutheran theology, courageous innovative pastoral practice, and solid Word and Sacrament ministry. I urge you to read it and listen to the voices from the city and add your own voice and experience.

264 Great Outreach Ideas, by Joel D. Heck (Concordia)

Rev. Joel Heck has compiled an invaluable resource of outreach ideas for any congregation that is serious about putting the Great Commission in action. In less than one hundred pages, he offers ideas upon ideas, resources upon resources for the individual Christian and congregations who seriously seek to be obedient to the mandate of making disciples of all nations.

The Jesus Enterprise: Engaging Culture to Reach the Unchurched, by Kent R. Hunter (Abingdon)

According to one reviewer, in this book the Rev. Kent Hunter outlines theologically, practically, "relevantly and realistically how to communicate the Gospel in today's society." Rev. Hunter gives example upon example of how this is being done by congregations in many cities and communities across America.

12 Pillars of a Healthy Church, by Waldo Werning (Fairway Press)

Rev. Werning's books are always a must read. He is a clear and concise thinker when it comes to the wholistic stewardship of the Christian and the church. His *12 Pillars of a Healthy Church* is biblical, Lutheran, Christian, and practical. He seeks in this volume, as well as his other books, to make the church a life-giving church and center for missionary formation.

The book lists Christian books, Web sites, and other resources that will help any congregation that seeks to enhance its mission and ministry assessment in serving the community.

Other Resources

1. *Demographic study of your community*. This will allow you to assess the demographics of your community in determining the size, age, household, income, and other pertinent information needed in serving people who oftentimes have specific needs.

2. *Strategic Planning Workshop*. This is a workshop that can be accessed from many district, synodical, and independent agencies that will help congregations in bolstering their mission statement, vision statement, core values, critical targets, objectives, and action plans for maximum outreach potential.

3. *Congregation Survey Resource*. This is an instrument that helps the congregation survey its own mission and ministry needs.

4. *Community canvassing*. Last but not least among reaching people is the tried, tested, and true method of canvassing your community on

a regular basis. The best way to get to know people and be known by them is to engage them regularly. Community canvassing has always proved to be a valuable tool for such awareness.

5. *Congregation Outreach Survey* provided by Roosevelt Gray.

How well does your church reach out to its community? Are you ready to welcome visitors? Take this simple quiz to find out where your church ranks in its ability effectively to welcome and connect the unchurched.

Choose the answer that most closely matches where your church is NOW.

Vision

1. The desire to reach lost people in our community is included in our Core Values, which influence our decisions, drive our ministry, and help us set priorities.

_____ Not True _____ Partly True _____ Mostly True _____ Completely True

2. My church has a clear, written vision statement that pictures our desired future.

_____ Not True _____ Partly True _____ Mostly True _____ Completely True

3. We have a mission statement that describes who we want to reach, what their needs are, and how we do ministry.

_____ Not True _____ Partly True _____ Mostly True _____ Completely True

4. Our church has completed a spiritual and demographic analysis of our target group and can describe the community's hopes, fears, and values.

_____ Not True _____ Partly True _____ Mostly True _____ Completely True

5. Our core group is well versed in the church's mission and vision and they enthusiastically support it with their time and energy.

_____ Not True _____ Partly True _____ Mostly True _____ Completely True

Strategy

6. My church plans outreach events such as special events, guest speakers, and topical sermon series.

_____ Not True _____ Partly True _____ Mostly True _____ Completely True

7. We have a clearly defined ministry plan that includes event promotion, personal networking, and direct mail.

_____ Not True _____ Partly True _____ Mostly True _____ Completely True

8. We have an easy-to-navigate website with its own domain name that closely matches the name of the church. It provides essential information about us and clearly communicates our identity.

_____ Not True _____ Partly True _____ Mostly True _____ Completely True

9. We regularly invite our target audience to church events.

_____ Not True _____ Partly True _____ Mostly True _____ Completely True

10. Our church has a paid or volunteer outreach director overseeing an outreach team.

_____ Not True _____ Partly True _____ Mostly True _____ Completely True

11. My church has allocated funds for local outreach programs, events, and tools.

_____ Not True _____ Partly True _____ Mostly True _____ Completely True

Programs

12. Attenders of my church are greeted by smiling people of various ages and nationalities.

____ Not True ____ Partly True ____ Mostly True ____ Completely True

13. Attenders are asked to fill out information forms.

____ Not True ____ Partly True ____ Mostly True ____ Completely True

14. Attenders are contacted after their visit by phone, letter, or thank-you card.

____ Not True ____ Partly True ____ Mostly True ____ Completely True

15. Attenders can get to know us by reading attractive and informative brochures.

____ Not True ____ Partly True ____ Mostly True ____ Completely True

16. We have a plan for integrating newcomers and a team of people to implement the plan.

____ Not True ____ Partly True ____ Mostly True ____ Completely True

17. We provide quality child care and Sunday School activities for children and a youth program for teens.

____ Not True ____ Partly True ____ Mostly True ____ Completely True

18. We make our worship service "user friendly" for newcomers.

____ Not True ____ Partly True ____ Mostly True ____ Completely True

Structure

19. Our building is well maintained and attractive.

_____ Not True _____ Partly True _____ Mostly True _____ Completely True

20. Our entrance is visible from the street and well marked.

_____ Not True _____ Partly True _____ Mostly True _____ Completely True

21. We have designated parking for visitors.

_____ Not True _____ Partly True _____ Mostly True _____ Completely True

22. We have an information booth or table where attenders can learn more about our church and programs.

_____ Not True _____ Partly True _____ Mostly True _____ Completely True

23. Our leadership structure is designed to facilitate outreach through a minimum of red tape and a clear priority to outreach.

_____ Not True _____ Partly True _____ Mostly True _____ Completely True

24. Our outreach team has a budget for advertising, direct mail, and other tools and can easily access the funds.

_____ Not True _____ Partly True _____ Mostly True _____ Completely True

Barriers to Outreach

25. Newcomers are not easily confused, but are directed to parking, classrooms, and worship services with clear, easy-to-read signs.

_____ Not True _____ Partly True _____ Mostly True _____ Completely True

26. Newcomers are not embarrassed by being asked to identify themselves by standing, raising their hand, or wearing a special nametag, but they are provided ways to get involved.

_____ Not True _____ Partly True _____ Mostly True _____ Completely True

27. Newcomers are not treated as strangers, but are warmly welcomed by current members who have been assigned to the task or respond naturally.

_____ Not True _____ Partly True _____ Mostly True _____ Completely True

28. Newcomers are not expected to find the church only on their own, but are actively invited to attend by their church friends who have been trained to use specially designed invitations.

_____ Not True _____ Partly True _____ Mostly True _____ Completely True

29. Newcomers are not pressured to make donations, but are verbally exempted during the collection.

_____ Not True _____ Partly True _____ Mostly True _____ Completely True

30. Newcomers are not limited to a single point-of-entry, but are given multiple entry points in addition to our Sunday service, such as special events, women's group, small groups, children's programs, and fine arts programs.

_____ Not True _____ Partly True _____ Mostly True _____ Completely True

Scoring

Add up your points for each category based on the following scale:

Each Not True = 0

Each Partly True = 1

Each Mostly True = 2

Each Completely True = 3

Add all your points together to get your final results.

Results

0–30 points: You need to take a hard look at your church's commitment to outreach. Your church needs to start fresh and set new visions and goals to make newcomers feel welcome.

30–60 points: Your church is on the road to being outreach friendly. Look back over your lower scores and see what areas need improvement—with some simple changes you can make a huge difference in your ability to reach the unchurched!

60–90 points: Your church is already outreach friendly, but there may be room for improvement. Invest your time and efforts into raising your lowest scores and you should see an improvement in your outreach efforts!

Reaching Hispanics
in the United States

Mark Junkans
Executive Director, LINC-Houston, Houston, Texas

Introduction

The Hispanic community is the fastest growing ethnic group in the United States and will soon become the country's largest ethnic group. Just to give a picture of how fast, for every Anglo that dies in the United States, 0.9 persons take their place. For every African American that dies, 1.9 persons take their place. But for every Hispanic that dies in the United States, 13 people take their place. Throughout the country, increasing numbers of Hispanics are living, working, and raising families. The United States is now the fifth largest Spanish-speaking country in the world. In Iowa, for example, in the last five to ten years, the most common language spoken among the dairy farmworkers has changed from English to Spanish. My brother-in-law in Iowa, who works for a veterinary pharmaceutical company, is trying to learn Spanish so that he can get better feedback from those who daily work with the dairy cows. There are small towns and cities throughout the Southeast whose populations have grown significantly because of the need for labor in new businesses.

As the Hispanic population increases, so does the general population throughout the United States, and many marketing firms have taken notice. What was once a small niche market has become more of a core market for major retail and commercial companies. Many marketing firms now talk about the Hispanic dollar and its great purchasing potential.

Coca-Cola and Pepsi battle it out with ads that hope to capture the Hispanic market. Ford and Chevy both try to sell themselves as the truck for the Hispanic community. American business has definitely taken notice. According to a July 2002 story in *The Dallas Morning News*, Latinos had more buying power in 2002 than the total for the state of Texas. And that buying power continues to grow at nearly three times the rate of the Caucasian population (story by Dianne Solis, July 28, 2002).

Hispanics live in the city, in the suburb, and in the small towns. They live in the expensive communities and in the barrios. A couple of decades ago in Houston, for example, most Hispanic immigrants moved first to the traditional Hispanic communities and then eventually found a better life in the outer parts of town. Today many are moving straight to the suburbs. While gateway cities like Houston and Los Angeles were once the first stop for all Hispanic immigrants coming to the United States, today cities like Atlanta, Georgia; Charlotte, North Carolina; and Lexington, Nebraska, are also now first stops. Hispanics are also taking more prominent roles in movies, pop charts, and politics. The author Richard Rodriguez referred to this demographic change as the "Browning of America."

No matter what our view of the causes for such an increased Hispanic population, the fact remains that they are the nation's fastest growing ethnic group, and as Dr. Esaul Solomon states, they are a "Great Harvest Waiting."

WHO ARE THE HISPANICS?

While we cannot exactly define the term Hispanic, we can generally define it for use in this chapter. According to the dictionary, the word *Hispanic* indicates something related to Spanish-speaking people or their culture or someone who can trace his or her origins to Spain or Latin America (or the culture). Thus Hispanic Americans are those who are of Spanish or Latin American descent, but were born in or are citizens of the United States. The word *Latino(a)* identifies someone born in or a citizen of a Latin American country and is often used to identify those of Latin American descent who were born in or who are citizens of the United States. In Spanish, *hispano* means "relating to Spain." In Latin America, people are never asked to state their race or ethnicity when filling out forms, so they only learn they are "Hispanic" upon crossing the United States border. Today in American English, the terms Latino and Hispanic are pretty much interchangeable, but there are Hispanic or Latino individuals who prefer one or the other.

Characteristics of Hispanic Culture

The Hispanic community, in general, could be characterized by its values. Hispanics tend to place a high value on relationships and on family. *Familia* (family) can mean both the nuclear family and the extended family. Extended family includes cousins, in-laws, *padrinos* (godparents), and good friends. Normally, if a person is considered part of the family, then he or she is automatically invited to any family functions. In fact, it is normally that person's obligation to be at those functions, except under extreme situations. The importance of family often affects decisions that an individual will make. For example, a son or daughter might pass up a job promotion if it would require a move to a different city or state away from family.

The importance placed on relationships also affects the way in which Hispanics view time. It would normally be more important to stay talking with someone who is visiting your house than to leave in time to make it to a meeting or a gathering. It is better in the Hispanic community to save face with the person to whom you are speaking than to shut down the conversation simply to arrive somewhere on time. Late arrival is forgivable, while sharply ending a conversation with someone with whom you are talking might not be. A Hispanic generally places importance on living life rather than working (they are most often not synonymous). A typical Hispanic might view his or her job as a necessary means to make an income so that life can be spent with loved ones and friends. To understand the Hispanic culture, one must understand a completely different system of values that affect every aspect of how life is lived and how responsibilities are prioritized.

Diversity among Hispanics

Many people are only familiar with one or two Hispanic groups, depending on their circle of contacts. Some might even say that if they have met one Hispanic then they have met them all. The truth is that it is hard to define the "Hispanic" group exactly because it is a label given to a large and diverse group of people living in the United States. They come from over twenty different countries, and within those same countries, there are unique people groups with their own distinct traditions, customs, languages, and histories. You could use the Spanish language as the thread that connects all Hispanics in America, but about half of the Hispanic population in the United States does not use Spanish as its primary language, and probably about a third or more cannot effectively communicate in Spanish at all. Naturally, Spanish-speakers tend to be more recent immigrants. The Hispanics for whom English is the dominant language are usually second- and third-generation immigrants. There are no absolutes in this because much depends on how a person was raised and how much time was spent in the school system in the United States. In *Language Choice in Hispanic-Background Junior High School Students in Miami: A 1998 Update*, researchers Barbara Zurer Pearson and Arlene McGee point out that though 40 percent of U.S. Hispanics are immigrants, by the third generation, they will probably not speak Spanish because of "increased cultural assimilation."

Goals and Objectives of My Ministry

In reaching out to Hispanics, as with any other ethnic group, the main goal for my ministry is to bring them to Christ and grow the kingdom. With that goal in mind, I focus on several specific objectives. The first objective is to plant new mission congregations where people can grow in faith and be nurtured through Word and Sacrament. The second is to meet the physical and felt needs of the individual and of the community so that they learn to trust our message. A third objective is to identify and equip leaders who can serve in community ministry and as leaders in the newly forming mission plants. These are not necessarily in chronological order, but often work themselves out simultaneously and congruently to grow the kingdom most effectively.

Mission Planting

I believe that the best way to reach new people is to plant new missions. Especially where language and culture are a barrier, the new mission plant has the advantage over the existing congregation. The new mission can speak a new language, adapt quickly to the surrounding culture, and from the beginning look like those living in the surrounding community.

It takes a lot of work to change the culture and attitude of an existing congregation, whereas a brand-new mission grows with its own personality and style from the beginning.

The first thing needed for a new mission is what I call "guerrilla evangelism." The church planter or church planting team begins to saturate an area with the Gospel through witness and relationships. Persistence and passion for the lost ultimately pay off when it comes to personal evangelism. The most effective evangelists I have seen in the Hispanic community are those who simply keep coming back with the same message of God's love in Jesus. They will try almost anything and sacrifice almost anything in order to bring the message of Christ to a community. They continue to share the Gospel and look for evidence of the Holy Spirit working in the heart of the individual. When someone seems to respond and desire more, then more intense focus is placed on that person. Leaving postcards, brochures, etc., is a nonthreatening way of sharing your faith with someone, but it is also almost noneffective in the Hispanic community. Relationships are built person-to-person, face-to-face. The Hispanic person values relationships over almost anything else, so evangelism must be relational. I will explain more about tools for evangelism when speaking about meeting needs, but the basic point here is that the evangelist must present the Gospel message clearly and consistently and with confidence for the witness to be effective.

In mission planting, we usually begin with home fellowships before anything else. When, through evangelism and relationships, we find a family who is open to the Gospel, we ask them if we can come back and share a Bible teaching with them. Usually we focus on faith topics and spiritual issues, like how to pray or how faith works. We also explain the Gospel clearly each time so that little by little they begin to understand God's grace in their lives. We encourage them to invite a friend or neighbor to their house the second time so that the friend may be blessed as well. It is much easier to begin with family units in the Hispanic community than to try to gather people in a single location. This is a lot of work for the mission planter, but people are more likely to come to a friend's home than a strange place like the church. An important part of the meeting is praying specifically for the needs in the family and those in attendance. People's faith begins to build when they learn to pray and trust God to help them in their particular situation. In subsequent meetings, we review the prayer requests made and ask how they saw God work in that situation. Many times, there has already been a direct answer to prayer by the time of the next meeting, which serves to solidify the family's perceived need for God. These meetings do not have to be every week, but can be held at any interval that works for the family's schedule. The main point is to minister to them directly, personally, and persistently. I have seen many churches grow from a simple house fellowship that eventually just outgrew the living room. A mission planter that works with several groups throughout a community will be forming disciples even before meeting for any formal worship.

Eventually, the group or groups get to a point where they are ready for formal worship. While it is tempting to just open the doors of the church from the beginning and invite people to worship, this is generally not an effective way to grow the church. You can expect only one or two families to show up at the beginning, unless you have been growing disciples prior to this through small fellowships and Bible studies. A church that has only one open door from the beginning, that is, public worship, will struggle for a long time just to get a core group in worship. People show up and wonder what is wrong with this church that only has a few people in it. They are probably used to churches in their home country that are overflowing with people.

Just because people tell you that they will be there when you invite them does not mean that they are coming. In the Hispanic culture it is very rare that someone will directly tell you no, unless he uses Catholicism as a reason. He may say, "I am already Catholic." You might respond by saying "I'm not trying to change your religion. I just want to help you know God's love better." Many will seem excited to come and tell you that they will be there, only to not show up when the hour comes. This is normal in most Hispanic cultures here in the United States with a few exceptions among different ethnic groups, such as Caribbean and South American people. I have often invited a family to worship or Bible study with an agreement from them, reminded them throughout the week, and even offered to pick them up only to find that when I got there, they had made other plans.

Remember that in the majority of Hispanic culture, *yes does not always mean yes*. In the Mexican and Central American culture, it is usually more offensive to tell someone "no" to his face than simply not to show up. You can bemoan this reality all day long, but it will not change the culture in which you are ministering. Many people do not make definite plans because, in their minds, they never know what will happen between now and that time. For example, they may have just received visitors and will not offend them by telling them to get out of the house so that the family can go to church. The son or father might take the car at the last minute to go somewhere and leave the family stranded. All sorts of things get in the way of people going to church. The mission planter persistently and lovingly works with them to understand the need for a commitment to God in the action of attending worship and Bible study. Rather than chastising persons for not coming or for not living up to their commitment, we need to remember to encourage them to make their commitment to God a top priority, based on His commitment to them. Remember that until people feel that they are part of the church family, they will always have a greater *compromiso* to their friends and extended family. This is especially true for the strange mission planter who invites them to church for worship. The goal is to build the relationship to the point where there is a loyalty and commitment to God and His church which supersedes people's commitment to anything or anyone else. This takes time, and a person should expect to hear a lot of "yes's" that really mean "maybe" or "I will think about it." Be persistent in love.

Meeting Needs in Jesus' Name

Henry Ward Beecher said, "You never know till you try to reach them how accessible men are; but you must approach each man by the right door." While it is true that God works faith through the Word and Sacraments, it is also true that ministry in urban settings and among the poor requires much in the way of meeting needs. Jesus ministered to the whole person, not just to the spiritual need. A mission planter or a church that wants to reach the Hispanic community will soon find the evangelistic advantage of meeting needs. Such needs are anything from learning the English language, to understanding and adapting to American culture, to basic food and clothing. In our mission churches we have offered almost every ministry imaginable to the community including: English as Second Language (ESL) classes, computer training classes, sewing classes, guitar classes, financial counseling, legal and immigration counseling, citizenship classes, food and clothing assistance, children's toys for Christmas, Thanksgiving meals for the community, health fairs, job fairs, back-to-school activities, girls' and boys' clubs, and so forth. No matter what ministry we do to meet people's needs, the ministry itself is not the end goal. Bringing people into a relationship with Christ and His church is the goal. In everything, we begin with prayer, introduce ourselves as Christians, talk about spiritual issues and nurture relationships with those we are serving. In our ministry, we regularly experience multiple blessings from meeting community needs. First, those whose needs are being met in Jesus' name will begin to see the church as a source of help in all areas of life. The community at large begins to see the church as a blessing for that community and the church enjoys goodwill and a good name among even the secular community. There are those who will catch the vision that the church puts forward for blessing the community and will join in the ministry with it. Often, many gifted and compassionate people in a community will join in with the ministry that the church is doing, even if they do not initially attend church there. As people see the purity of heart on the part of the church and the joy in the volunteers, they will begin to wonder what exactly is going on. People often begin to say, "We come, and you pour yourselves into our lives. Who pays for all this?" As they see Christians volunteer their time and dedicate them-selves to the well-being of the community, they also begin to ask the question, "Why? Why is the church doing this?" The church answers that question with a resounding, "Because Christ has done as much for us."

Meeting people's needs opens doors to their hearts. In a Northwest area of Houston where we planned to start a new Hispanic mission, we began to walk the streets with flyers in hand, taking a spiritual survey of every single household. We got to know a lot of families and were even invited into a few houses for conversation. We were asking the question, "What is the greatest need of the Hispanic community here?" We also went to speak with school administrators and community leaders, asking the same question. We began to find that, even though there were other similar programs in the area, there was still a great need for ESL classes. We began a partnership with the Houston Public Library System's adult education department and soon had ESL classes running twice a week with about eighty students. Soon after, we began a soccer camp for chil-dren during the summer and held various other activities for the His-panic community. The difference in our reception at the houses we visited was like night and day after we had been meeting community needs. Prior to doing community ministry we were welcomed coldly by most of the homes and even after eight to ten visits had not made any significant headway into most households. After doing ministry that met community needs, it was a different story. We specifically went to visit those households that were involved in the program and their circle of friends. Almost every single house we visited now received us as family and spent considerable time talking about their lives and faith. We were able to share the Gospel in greater detail over a series of visits. Even the households that were not involved with the ministry were more receptive when we announced ourselves as the "church that has the ESL classes and soccer camp." While people do not automatically become worshipers at the church, it does at least open the door for presenting the Gospel friend-to-friend. The Bible classes and worship services began to grow slowly as a result of our Gospel ministry through meeting people's needs. This same scenario has played itself out in various situations across the city and God still gets the glory.

The most important thing to remember when meeting community needs is that the particular ministry that you are doing is not the end, it is the beginning of a relationship. It still takes great work to move people from coming to receive a service or training to becoming disciples of Jesus Christ. Many churches miss out on that fact when doing social ministry. They are willing to do the work of organizing people to meet a need but do not go the extra step to grow the kingdom through that ministry, or they lose patience while waiting for someone to respond. It takes an intentional, continual, and targeted Gospel message through relationships to build faith in people's hearts to the point where they begin to ask for Bible studies and worship.

Raising Up and Equipping Leadership

A key component to any ministry is the formation of leaders to carry out that ministry. When ministering to Hispanics, I tended to make two major mistakes again and again. The first was to underestimate people's need for contact with their leader. Let me explain. As a white boy who is very independent, I learned to function pretty much on my own. I come from a large family that loves each other but whose members can pretty much survive on their own. We are probably typical among North American Anglos in that regard. We are spread out across several states and many of us did not think twice about moving away from the family. Not so with the average Hispanic family. Families often stay in the same city, forsaking even job promotions, so that they can continue to be together on weekends and special occasions. In the church, I, as a self-dependent Anglo-Saxon pastor, tended to contact people only when there was a need to do so. I would prepare everything for Bible class and worship and visit those whom I needed to visit, but I left it at that. The problem with this is that there was not sufficient time for my faith to rub off on those I was serving so that they could become fully devoted disciples of Christ. I look at the Book of Acts and see a group of people that devoted themselves to being with each other. The apostles did not do ministry in a vacuum, but rather spent their time with those they were discipling, just at Jesus did. In North American pastoral training, we are often warned about becoming too friendly with the parishioners, with spending too much time with people. In the Hispanic church, this is generally not the case. It is important, however, for an outsider to remember that there are limits to how friendly one can be with the family, if one is not yet family. There are many unwritten rules of engagement in different Hispanic cultures that must be learned in order to avoid offense.

The second mistake I made was to put people into leadership positions too early and leave them alone to perform their function without adequate assistance. I could not understand why those I had identified as leaders wouldn't rise to the challenge when I would place them in a leadership position. Almost every time I put men in a leadership position in the church they would stop participating shortly after. Almost the opposite would happen with the women. As soon as one was placed in a leadership position she would either get henpecked by the other women or would soon become overbearing and demanding of the other women. Of course, this depends a lot on personality, but I definitely saw a trend forming. My mistake was putting individuals too quickly into leadership positions. The men usually ran away from what they knew as leadership. My reactionary solution was not to have any leadership positions in the church, but this is not a proper solution in any organization. My problem was that I did not build them up in various functions for an adequate time before I called them to be leaders. I began to ask people to perform tasks for me, starting with smaller tasks and building to larger ones. I would tell them that they could involve as much help as they needed to make it work, rather than putting all the pressure on them as individuals. I would also help them perform the tasks they were assigned, and then I celebrated the fact that they performed the task. This is a lot more hand holding than I'm used to doing. I want someone to just tell me what needs to be done and then let me do it. Not so with most of our men. Eventually, as their tasks become bigger and bigger, they begin to prove themselves as leaders without even knowing it. Their tasks require greater help from others, and I can see their capabilities of organizing people for ministry. Before they know it, they are in leadership positions, but are not publicly or privately called leaders. The entire burden for having the title of leader rests on my shoulders until they come to the conclusion that they actually are called to be leaders as well. This slow process takes a lot of persistence and patience on the part of the mission planter. I cannot fully develop this point with the space provided; other Hispanic cultures are different in this regard. Among Panamanians and Puerto Ricans, for example, I have found that generally people thrive more on leadership titles than they do among Mexican and other Central American communities. The point is to know the community in which you are ministering and become familiar with the leadership styles used in that society.

When I have walked alongside some persons for a while and they have begun to perform greater tasks for the church with more reliability, I begin to prepare them for more spiritual leadership in the church. This comes through Bible studies, training courses and more dedicated time spent with individuals to build their faith and confidence in what God is calling them to do. A natural step from doing tasks might be to begin to teach a class or to be a prayer leader for worship or house fellowships. Spiritual leadership must come in stages as the person sees more and more how God wants to use him in ministry according to his gifts, and as he becomes more like Christ. Moving a person into leadership too quickly can lead to frustration and disaster, but waiting too long to let them loose can also stifle not only their growth but also ultimately the ministry. As soon as I had a solid Hispanic spiritual leader in place, my purpose was to exit the church as quickly as possible. The longer I stayed the less freedom that leader felt to do things his way. As I got out of the way, that individual began to lead with a very personal and nurturing style and slowly built up a team of leaders from among the congregation. They did everything together and met continually as a leadership team to reinforce what each other was doing. I learned more from my successor than he ever learned from me concerning leadership. Instead of one white guy trying to keep the mission church going, there is a healthy body of leaders that prepare for and lead worship, teach Bible classes, lead children's ministry, and organize community ministry through the community center.

Worship in the Hispanic Church

Worship style in the Hispanic church is as varied as it is in our North American churches. Some churches have a liturgical style, while others have adopted a modern contemporary style. No matter what style, the fact is that Hispanic worship is more community oriented and flexible. The number one goal I had at the beginning was to start worship service on time. I generally liked to wait until a good size group was there to begin. This ultimately meant that we would begin later and later. Punctuality is a moving target, but not generally a priority. Ending time for the worship is not as crucial either. The fact that the church gathers together as a family to worship God and receive from Him is most important. Many details that are noticed in North American Anglo churches go unnoticed in the Hispanic church. It is not so much a lack of excellence, but rather excellence in different areas. One thing that worship must be in the Hispanic community is passionate. There is no room today in the Hispanic community for dry, stale worship that simply goes through the motions. The mission planter must learn to let loose a little when leading worship and allow people to participate as much as possible. Worship is more celebratory, noisy, and free in the Hispanic church. Therefore learn to embrace the seeming chaos and place a value on people over performance, community over execution.

Lutheran Theology

Many readers may wonder how we do this kind of outreach in a new culture and still maintain our Lutheran theology and heritage. The simplistic answer is, "The same as we've always done it." This is true and yet not true at the same time. We do continue in a rich heritage that has been ours throughout many years. We place a high degree of importance on the correct division of Law and Gospel, the Sacraments, and on grace. We do not compromise our theological stance on issues such as abortion, women's role in ministry, and veneration of saints. What may be different in our approach is the willingness to do whatever it takes, within scriptural boundaries, to win our communities for the kingdom. The Holy Spirit is the one who converts and gives us the power to do anything positive for the kingdom. He has given us a wealth of gifts, talents, and resources to use for His purposes and we are more than eager to use them to their fullest potential. While we have a definite stance on doctrinal issues, we also know that individuals will take time to come to a maturity of faith and biblical understanding. That requires some flexibility on our part as we strive to equip leaders for ministry. If a person is faithful in leading a group, he is then trained for spiritual leadership. If he continues to be faithful and effective, he is then placed in theological training through one of the seminary programs, such as the Ethnic Immigrant Institute of Theology or the Hispanic Institute of Theology, which ultimately leads toward ordination in our church body. Lay leaders who help to plant new missions do so under the supervision of a local ordained pastor.

Conclusion

Ministry among Hispanics in North America can be both exciting and agonizing, as is the case with any group of people. There can be great frustration when people do not react as we believe they should. Things may not move as quickly as we would like, people may not respond as enthusiastically to our message as we would hope, and it often takes a long time to build commitment. There is also great joy in ministry among Hispanics. The sense of community and family worshiping and working together for the kingdom are incredible as a ministry builds momentum. There is huge potential for the kingdom as the Hispanic population grows throughout North America. How will the church respond?

MUSLIM OUTREACH MINISTRY

Khurram Khan
Executive Director of People of the Book Lutheran Outreach,
Dearborn Heights, Michigan

As the United States continues to manifest its multicultural nature, people are experiencing drastic change in their neighborhoods. Individuals from all over the world can be seen in the shopping mall, the workplace, businesses, and in educational institutions. Students from around the world are prominent in professional education programs at U.S. institutions and are competing in all areas of excellence. This reminds us that God has provided tremendous opportunity to learn more about other cultures and religions. God always provides the availability and desires that we take the initiative and share the Gospel message courageously.

Approximately one billion people today are Muslims, and Islam is the fastest growing religion by birth in the world, with around six million adherents in the United States alone. Islam teaches that all Muslims, all one billion, are to be missionaries; they are to find an opportunity to convert non-Muslims to Islam. By doing so, Muslims believe they will win the right to enter paradise. Thus they take this opportunity seriously, with obvious results. Each year more than seven thousand Muslim men marry American women and convert them to Islam. The children born through these marriages are raised as Muslims. The high birthrate in Muslim communities and family sponsorship in the immigration program rapidly increase the number of Muslims in the United States. About ten thousand students come to the United States for higher education, and 80 percent make the United States their permanent home. When one immigrant becomes a citizen of the United States, the family sponsorship program means the individual can sponsor parents, siblings and their spouses, and dependent children. Thus the Muslim population will continue to grow.

Statistics show that each Muslim who dies will leave ten behind, all sponsored by one person. There is only one option: The church needs to open the doors and welcome not only Muslims but Hindus, Sikhs, Buddhists, and all others, evangelizing and teaching them Christian theology and responding to their questions.

Islam teaches its followers that the conversion of one non-Muslim to Islam will result in a handsome reward from Allah—sins will be forgiven and a mansion will be allotted to him in paradise. This incentive makes each Muslim an active evangelist. You may notice that the moment you begin a conversation with a Muslim, he will be quick to ask whether you are Muslim. From that day, no opportunity will be missed to talk about Islam. The ultimate goal will be to convert you to Islam.

All Christians are to be reminded of Matthew 28:19. The Great Commission is for every Christian, and we are to be ready at all times to witness to the message of hope and salvation through Christ to Muslims and to all others living in the community. Our Lord and Savior issued the Great Commission, but why are Christians not ready to move forward and share the Gospel message with nonbelievers? It is difficult to approach a foreigner when we lack knowledge of other religions or cultures. Such an effort requires courage and training. But we can comfortably say that the church has developed quite a number of resources to help us understand other cultures, including Eastern religions. Most important, we should have sufficient knowledge of our own Scriptures. If we are weak in the knowledge of our own Scriptures, beliefs, and practices, we do not stand a chance to evangelize others. Ideally, we can make new contacts, then connect them with a pastor or a missionary. Then you have done a wonderful job by bringing your friends or co-workers to the right place and introducing them to a pastor or missionary who is trained and understands cultural sensitivities.

American Muslims come from all over the world: Africa, the Middle East, South and East Asia, Europe, and of course people born in the Americas. Thus there are hundreds of subcultures within Islam. It would be useful to know the basic information of each subculture. One can learn about the culture by asking questions, which not only provides a reason to communicate but also puts the other person at ease and provides encouragement to give you maximum information about his or her culture. Most ethnic groups are proud of their heritage and culture. They will always feel important if someone is interested in learning about their traditions or rituals and culture.

There are about seventy-two sects within Islam. The major sects are Sunni, Shiites, and Wahabi. These sects may unify in the face of a common enemy, but they do not pray together under one roof. Muslims in the United States and Europe represent all these sects. In an initial conversation, a Muslim will not talk about the other sects. Instead, he will try to portray an image of being united under Islam. Islam is a traditional religion. Muslims today have all the traditions of Muhammad in written form and follow these traditions. In many cases, traditions of Muhammad are the final law that governs the Islamic society. Muslims are active in countries in which they are in the minority to get concessions for Islamic law to be enforced for the Muslim community. Islam is a male-dominated religion. This has been a political struggle in Europe, and that struggle has moved into the Canadian parliament as well.

Islam produces well-educated people in all areas of excellence. You will find professionals in each field of business, science, and technology. Muslims are an important element in the fabric of the global society and they contribute a lot.

One thing that has not changed in 1,400 years is that Muslims tend to create a society within the society. Their demand to have a separate state-sponsored and state-funded school system is another issue to be addressed. I think that if cultural barriers are removed and bridges are built within communities, this will not only bring people together, but it will also help build trust among us and the people of other religions. Past experience taught us that the melting-pot theory of U.S. social development has failed. People may change their religion, but they will not change their cultures and traditions. What they value most is the traditions of their forefathers. Even in advanced civilizations, people are not ready to compromise in this area.

This leaves one door open for development: reaching the unreached. The church has been remiss with the Great Commission for hundreds of years. Fourteen hundred years ago, if only the orthodox churches in the Middle East had opened their doors to the pagans of Arabia or if they had made some effort to translate the Bible into Arabic so the pagans could read the message of the cross, millions would have been saved from going to hell. The church cannot afford to put evangelism on the back burner if it wishes to avoid repeating past mistakes, whether in the present or future.

God has a plan for every Muslim who lands in the United States. The church has to prepare a comprehensive outreach program to meet the new challenges. Many denominations have not yet opened their doors for indigenous leadership. Without indigenous leadership, it is difficult to start ministries. Language and cultural barriers become the biggest road-blocks in sharing the Good News of Jesus Christ. Resource material to be used for evangelism is another important factor. In the two thousand years of our history, the church needed additional resources for reaching the lost with the Gospel message of love.

Islam is growing and will continue to grow more because of the weak-ness of the church and the ignorance of many who do not see the oppor-tunity in their backyard. People are living side by side with Muslims and may never have communicated a word of encouragement to each other. Many opportunities arrive each day to reduce the distance and grasp the chance to communicate the message of forgiveness of sins through the cross. If only one will open the door of his house and invite Muslims to spend some time sharing their experiences in this country. A few words of encouragement from us can mean a lot to a new immigrant or a refugee family that has recently arrived in the neighborhood.

OBJECTIVE

The objective of People of the Book Outreach Ministry is primarily to reach Muslims and to identify and train indigenous leaders. We want to empower and prepare these leaders by the Word of God to share the Good News of Jesus Christ in the language of their hearts, with the end result of making disciples (Matthew 28:9–20) and planting healthy Christ-cen-tered congregations.

GOALS

The main goal is to bring those who do not know Jesus to become the members of His body. We need to have different strategies to meet the needs of each person. Since every situation is unique, strategies or techniques keep on changing from community to community. Each setting has a different strategy. For example, one program may not be needed or effective at another outreach ministry site. It depends upon the community itself; if the community is from a country where the education standard is low, then educational institutes will draw the most immigrants. The same cannot be applied to the European Muslim community, as it is already well educated.

Therefore setting up strategies to achieve the goals requires a lot of research. Research can begin with in-person interviews, which can be conducted in homes and businesses. Surveys should include both parents and children. A team of people, with volunteer spirit and gifts, is to be selected to plan strategy and execute the outreach effort. They will have to use different models of human care ministries to earn the right to be heard within each community. This team should be from the community where the work is to be conducted. In this way, they will know the needs of the new families and the opportunities available for assistance. The team must have at least 50 percent women, otherwise the program will be a failure. The number of women in the Muslim community is 52 percent. Culture does not allow men to communicate with women openly. Therefore it is not by choice, but by necessity that we include women missionaries in the team. These women can easily visit homes and pick up and drop off Muslim women to and from the programs. We have experienced a fast growth in the ministry where female workers have been deployed to work side by side with the male missionary-pastors.

POBLO is an outreach movement at the cutting edge; we are face-to-face with those people who need to get one chance in their lifetime to hear the Gospel. Thousands of Muslims are dying each day without hearing the message. Every Christian is responsible for one lost soul that dies in sin without hearing the message of hope and salvation through Jesus Christ. POBLO is working hard to carry the burden with limited resources. We need to pray that God may open the hearts of believers that they start praying for the Muslims to be saved. Some of the strategies that have been very effective in opening the doors for witnessing are listed below.

Indigenous Worker

Due to the language and culture barrier, it is highly important for the church to identify and encourage indigenous leaders within the church.

Ethnic membership should be encouraged at all times and at all the parishes. Church leadership should promote the cause of raising ethnic workers and sending them to the seminary or training institutes to increase their knowledge. Institutes should be ready to give free education to those who are committing their lives to serve the Lord as missionaries to the Muslims or others. Unless the church body will invest time, effort, and finances to train ethnic workers, there will be no advancement in outreach to Muslims. Solid theological training is the first and most important step toward starting the ministry to Muslims.

Equipping workers with tools to evangelize is the second important requirement for outreach ministry. Some resources are available and more can be produced. But the most important tool is strong communication skills. Not every person has these gifts, but those who are willing to learn can do much better once they complete their training. POBLO Ministries have found out with experience that if a missionary is weak in taking initiative, then he is definitely weak in communications as well. A missionary has to have the ability to communicate the Gospel message in the most effective way to the elderly, young adults, and children. One never knows who will open the heart to the message first.

Knowledge of Scripture

Our goal is to train indigenous leaders by sending them to the seminary for education and ministry experience. It is important for an outreach worker to have a solid knowledge of Scripture along with the ability to relate the Bible to the subject being discussed. If the teacher is weak in understanding the Word of God, then he cannot succeed in reaching others.

Every Muslim starts reading the Qur'an at the age of four. The Qur'an has four chapters that talk about Mary and Jesus, the Messiah. These chapters of the Qur'an present the miracles of Jesus, His virgin birth, and His second coming. But, beyond these common points, the Qur'an presents a distorted story that is different from the Bible. The Qur'an also attacks the Bible by claiming it is changed and therefore corrupted. Not only has Islam failed to support this claim, but the Dead Sea Scrolls prove exactly the opposite. Even so, Muslims steadfastly hold that the Bible has been corrupted. This makes the job of a missionary difficult; he has to be well versed in the knowledge of the Christian Scriptures and the application of the verses. He or she should be able to defend the Scriptures and explain the Bible to the other person.

Knowledge of the Culture

All missionaries should be well acquainted with the culture of the community with which they work. A Muslim community may be African, Middle Eastern, Afghani, Iranian, Pakistani, Malaysian, or Russian. All have their own culture and separate traditions. Even the food of each community is unique. Language also separates communities from each other. One Muslim from Afghanistan has to learn English to communicate with another Muslim from Pakistan or Jordan. This fact places great importance on the English language and presents English-speaking people with an opportunity to teach their own culture, as well as to learn from others about their non-English culture. Before approaching a Muslim community it is always wise to read more about the culture of that community. The missionary can go to a public library and read a few books about the particular country from which these people come. Another great resource is the Internet, with its vast amount of freely available information. A third option, available for LCMS members, is POBLO Ministries. Call POBLO and they will conduct a workshop to provide information about the Islamic culture and particularly about the Muslim community that you plan to reach.

Making Contacts

The first task is to make new contacts within the community. By visiting shopping malls, grocery stores, and vegetable markets, we can make new contacts. In a first encounter, you can ask some nonthreatening questions that invite dialogue:

"How long have you been living in the United States?"

"Do you like this country?"

"How is your family back home?"

"Do you intend to bring your family to the United States?"

"Will you let me know if I can be of any assistance to you or your family?"

"May I pray for your health and your needs?"

Every missionary should go into the mission field and make new contacts every week. This will increase your list of people who can join various programs designed to help the community and also educate them more about the culture and life in the United States. All POBLO missionaries start their day with making new contacts. Our goal is to connect with each individual living in the neighborhood.

English as a Second Language (ESL)

Every Muslim is not highly educated to the level of having good command of the English language. Especially Middle Eastern Muslims have to go through the language learning process. New immigrants often work in factories or take small jobs. To be able to be accepted by a factory or business, they must have English language skills. Therefore they are looking for a place close to their home or a few minutes' drive for education in a comfortable and casual setting. For the sake of learning the language, Muslims will not hesitate to come to the church building. Reading, writing, and speaking skills are their needs. The Lutheran Church is second only to Roman Catholics in education; we have thousands of retired teachers who are willing to volunteer a few hours a week. ESL teaching courses are available; training is available upon request. In POBLO'S experience, this has been the most effective way of evangelizing Muslims.

Immigration and Refugee Services

Immigrants and refugees need lots and lots of help in their paperwork processing. In the first place they do not have enough money to pay for the services required. Second, they do not possess language skills. Third, the system is new for them. New immigrants often depend on someone from their culture who is more educated and has the contacts to get the job done. Therefore any type of service ministry will draw not single individuals, but masses of people to itself. We have this program at our five POBLO locations and are planning to provide these services at all the ministry stations.

Food and Clothing Bank

The practical needs of immigrants are many and resources are limited. Providing a food supply is a big help to families. Refugee families are generally large families and they require more food than a typical nuclear

Anglo family. The church can offer free food once or twice a month; the only precaution is not to offer or distribute pork products, which are taboo for Muslims, as they are for Jews.

A clothing bank is essential to assimilating Muslim women into American society. Given their limited finances, women will accept free clothing and start wearing American styles that do not conflict with Muslim sensibilities. Not only is this economical for the family, but it also makes it a little easier for the women to move around less conspicuously in their adopted society.

Children and Youth Programs

Children are anxious and eager to play new games and have fun. Muslim youth struggle between two cultures, as they are part of the western culture at their school, and as soon as they come home they are surrounded by their traditional culture. Therefore it is important that they can participate in various games and youth activities. Churches and other Christian organizations can arrange youth retreats and organized activities for the young people. Children and teenagers are very open and tend to form strong bonds with newfound friends; consequently, we have seen very good results from this type of activity. POBLO has a goal that the initial program it will create at every new ministry site is directed toward youth.

As in any outreach ministry where missionaries interact with people of other faith traditions and cultures, we are mindful of the possibility that our own theology may be compromised in the process. We believe that we do not sacrifice Lutheran theology as we develop the outreach ministry to Muslims. When we look at this issue, we ask two basic questions:

1. What is Lutheran theology?

2. What is outreach ministry?

Our Lutheran Confessions state: "Everything we need to believe as Christians is told to us in the Scriptures." We believe in the absolute authority of Scriptures. As Robert D. Preus explains it, (1) Scriptures are the one divine source from which, as from a spring or fountain, we draw all our theology; (2) Scriptures are the only authority to judge teachers and teachings in the church. The Confessions state what we Lutherans believe to be the teachings of Scripture and what we therefore believe, teach, and publicly confess are how all doctrines should be judged. Our beloved Lutheran Church confesses several fundamental things, according to Preus: (1) that Christ and His work of redemption is the basis for our justification, (2) that God justifies us freely by grace, and (3) that we receive God's justification and all its blessings through faith in Christ. Christ and His work of redemption is the basis for our justification, God justifies us freely by grace, and we receive God's justification and all its blessings through faith in Christ alone.

We believe that we receive grace through His Word, Baptism, and Lord's Supper. This grace comes with no qualification of ours, but it was all done on the cross. John 3:16 defines the unconditional nature of God's grace very clearly. When we look at 1 John 2:2, we see that Christ's atoning sacrifice was for the whole world, not for us alone.

Since Lutheran theology is based on Scripture, when we engage in outreach, we do not sacrifice Lutheran theology because outreach is nothing but carrying the saving message of the Gospel to those who do not know Jesus. Outreach ministry is purely what God commanded in Matthew 28:19–20.

Islam is a religion full of traditions and laws. It is a religion that believes in deeds. A Muslim can only reach heaven either through the will of Allah or through his or her good deeds. Second, Muslims do not allow non-Muslims in their place of worship, nor do they appreciate the presence of non-Muslims in their rituals or religious functions. We as Lutherans do not worship officially with nonbelievers, and we believe in closed Communion. We believe that anyone who receives the Lord's Supper in a Lutheran church should be instructed so that he or she may truly know the meaning of the words: "This is My body; this is My blood." Muslims do understand the exclusive nature of religious traditions because they come from a traditional Islamic background. Therefore we do not need to compromise on our belief.

If we do not compromise what the Scriptures tell us, then we are at the same time not compromising on the Lutheran theology. When we read the book *The Theology of the Cross for the Twenty-First Century* by Victor Raj, we learn that the theology of the cross "is a vivid example of a constructive missionary vision under the cross for global witness." Furthermore, the theology of the cross points to the reality that no one culture owns the Christian faith. The greatest insight of Luther's theology of the cross is that the cross reveals God Himself to us through His incarnate Son, Jesus Christ, who was crucified on the cross to save mankind.

This is the message that we carry each day into the streets, well defined in John 3:16. To all the faiths, beliefs, religions, cults, etc., that believe that only through works or deeds or virtues are we saved, we take the message of grace with a great excitement. It is not what we do that will take us to heaven, but it is through what Christ did on the cross that we will enter heaven. We as Christians continue to sin but His grace is sufficient for us. We are saved by the blood of Jesus. I once asked a Muslim, "How many good deeds are required to get you into heaven? Does your Qur'an give any specific number?" He said, "No." So if you do not know how many, then what's the assurance?

A young engineer from Yemen came to me for help. He wanted to marry a Christian girl, whose mother was determined that her daughter would only marry him if he became a Christian. His own parents told him they would excommunicate him if he converts to Christianity. He was walking on a fine line. His girlfriend's mother sent him to me. I asked him only two questions:

1. Why do you believe in a religion and what do you want to attain?

2. By practicing all five pillars of Islam and following all that you are taught, do you think at your last moment of life you would have the assurance of heaven?

The young man stood up, smiled, and said he had the answer—that only through grace and by faith in Jesus can we be saved.

Lutheran theology is never sacrificed while developing outreach ministry. I would say it is fulfilled and completed when we carry the Gospel to those who do not know Jesus and bring them to the body of Christ. Christ came for the lost—those who are sick, those who are of the other pen—so that there may be one flock and one shepherd. If Jesus had to come and die on the cross for the sins of the Muslims, Hindus, Sikhs, Bahis, and Buddhists, He would have still come. It is His desire that all are saved and none perish. It is absolutely essential and mandatory for our missionaries and workers to be worshiping LCMS Lutherans. There is no compromise on that. Further, we only admit converts from Islam and other religions into church membership after they have gone through a series of instruction classes.

Selected Resources We Use
to Facilitate Our Ministry

POBLO uses many resources to facilitate the ministry. First and foremost is the Bible. In our collection of resources, we have the Bible in about twenty-five languages. Then we have the Jesus video available in at least eighteen languages. We have prepared many brochures on various topics and keep in stock brochures that are written and prepared by many converts from Islam.

There are hundreds of books and booklets written by new converts along with their own testimonies. Any one of these printed materials is a very good tool to pass to a seeker. Five or six organizations are preparing resource materials for evangelism, and we make these materials available as needed. We also use Luther's Small Catechism printed in Arabic and Persian languages. It is our goal to translate and print it in at least fifty languages by the year 2017.

How We Consider Our Ministry Effective

The work of the field missionary is to plant the seed and pray for the fruits. The Holy Spirit brings good fruits. Our understanding of the effectiveness of the ministry is to plant the seed and pray for fruits. The Holy Spirit brings good fruits. Our understanding of the effectiveness of the ministry is to count the fruits. When people are baptized in the name of the Father, and the Son, and the Holy Spirit, new people are joining the body of Christ. When Muslims leave their families and choose to join our church, it gives us assurance that Christ is building His church. In 2004, 142 Muslims were baptized through POBLO'S National and International Ministries. These people are now members of Lutheran congregations. And we thank our Lord for using our ministry for His kingdom.

CHINESE AMERICAN OUTREACH MINISTRY

Shiu Ming Lau
Pastor of Lutheran Church of the Holy Spirit, San Francisco, California (Formerly Pastor of Light of Christ Lutheran Mission, St. Louis, Missouri)

INTRODUCTION

Lin, a young mother with three children, moved with her husband from China to New York City. After several years the family moved to St. Louis.

Lin came to Light of Christ Chinese Lutheran Mission (LOC) through the English as a Second Language program (ESL). She desired to improve her ability to use the English language. While attending the Sunday ESL class, a member of LOC invited her to stay for the worship service. Lin accepted the invitation.

The next week Lin, who does not drive a car, went grocery shopping. It normally took her twenty minutes to walk home. Pastor and Mrs. Shiu Ming Lau also went grocery shopping that day. On their return trip home, the Laus saw Lin walking, "lugging" her groceries home. They recognized her as the woman with three children who had worshiped at LOC the previous Sunday. When they stopped their car and offered to take her home, she accepted the offer; so they loaded her groceries into their van and drove her home.

After a number of weeks of home visitation and personal evangelism, the Holy Spirit changed Lin's heart. She enrolled in the adult confirmation class taught by Pastor Lau. The Holy Spirit worked faith in her heart. She and her three children are now baptized and regularly attend LOC.

Whenever Lin comes to Bible study, worship services, or ESL, her smile expresses the great joy she now has. Every Sunday, in the worship service, she sings very loudly and after Light of Christ's worship service she helps serve the fellowship meal. Lin says that this is one way that she can serve her Lord because of His wonderful grace.[1]

By 2000, the number of the Asian Americans grew to ten million, and those with Chinese ancestry account for about 24 percent. Yet many Chinese Americans are still outside of the church. They are still living in the realm of spiritual darkness. Light of Christ Lutheran Chinese Mission (LOC) was established at St. Louis in the year 2000. Its mission is very clear: **L**ove each other, **I**lluminated by Christ, **G**ive the **H**ope of salvation **T**o the Chinese (*Light*).

LOC is a young mission with a deep burden for the lost. There are about thirty-five thousand Chinese in the St. Louis metropolitan area alone.[2] LOC is now a Chinese mission under Immanuel Lutheran Church and financially subsidized by the Missouri District of the LCMS.

In this chapter, I want to share with readers the challenges and strategies of outreach and evangelism to Chinese Americans. Over the last couple of years, through contact with these Chinese Americans, LOC has accumulated some experience and understanding about how to share the Gospel effectively with them. This can be helpful to other Chinese ministries elsewhere.

Outreach and Evangelism to Chinese Americans

Difficulties

Outreach and evangelism to Chinese Americans are not easy for several reasons. First, the diversity of the Chinese churches is obvious. In

---

[1] This testimony is derived from a newsletter, which is prepared by my co-worker, the Rev. Ray Mirly, and sent to those who are supporting our ministry, Light of Christ Lutheran Chinese Mission.

[2] By census, the Chinese population is about 20,000. Yet an estimated 15,000 additional people are the invisible population. They are international students and their families; Chinese seniors, who are holding visiting or tourist visas, who come to help take care of the grandchildren while their sons and daughters are working to earn the living; restaurant workers who isolated themselves from the census survey due to the language barrier; and illegal immigrants.

bigger cities, Chinese churches can be divided by their language preference in the worship service. There are four different possible monolingual services: Cantonese, Mandarin, Taiwanese, or English. There are five kinds of bilingual services: English-Cantonese; English-Mandarin; Cantonese-Mandarin; English-Taiwanese; and Taiwanese-Mandarin. But in a smaller city, such as St. Louis, Mandarin is the official language for all Chinese churches. The Cantonese-speaking Chinese Americans can only choose English or Mandarin speaking churches since the majority of the Chinese in St. Louis are from Taiwan or mainland China. At LOC, we use Mandarin for our worship service and Bible study group. If someone does not speak Mandarin or English, he will probably remain among the lost because of the language barrier.

Educational background is the second difficulty for outreach to Chinese Americans. Because of the different levels of education, different outreach strategies are needed for Chinese professionals or intellectuals and laborers or restaurant workers. In the 1980s and 1990s, many Chinese churches began as Bible study groups on campus and focused on international students. Later, as some students found jobs in the local areas and settled down, the groups expanded to become formal churches. Many Chinese churches still focus on the international students, professionals, and intellectuals. However, the general church worship schedule might not fit the situation of the restaurant workers or laborers because these people work a long day every day, including Sunday. The church must design a special outreach strategy for their needs.

The third difficulty for an outreach to Chinese Americans is the tension between the overseas-born Chinese (OBC) and American-born Chinese (ABC). Except on the West Coast in cities such as San Francisco and Los Angeles, or on the East Coast in cities such as New York City and Boston, where we can see a fourth or fifth generation of Chinese, generally the age of Chinese Americans is about 30 to 65. Most of this age group is OBC. This group of Chinese Americans is a bread-winning group; they are trying to support whole families. In many Chinese churches, OBC fill leadership positions and are the pillars of the churches. With their income, they financially support the churches, and with their commitment they are guiding the direction of the churches. However, a new generation, the ABC, are gradually growing up. Because of differences in educational background and cultural understanding, there is some tension between the OBC and ABC.

In 2002, Chinese church workers and missionaries of the LCMS met at Houston, Texas, and studied the strategies for outreach to Chinese Americans. A guest speaker portrayed the difference between the OBC and ABC as follows: Overseas-born Chinese are a group of more conservative and traditional people; they are inward and noninvolved in the American culture; they are family oriented and relational; and they are more indirect, cautious, and desire to save face in any confrontation. American-born Chinese are more liberal and broad-minded. Socially speaking, ABC are more outward and involved, more aggressive, individualistic, and goal-oriented. They are also more direct, logical, and focused when in confrontational situations. ABC are generally weak in speaking their mother tongue since they were educated in English.

"The second generation is being lost." This is a comment by a multicultural church planter.[3] According to a survey done in the 1990s, only 4 percent of the ABC would choose to return to their parents' churches, the spiritual home where they grew up.[4] Once they leave, they neither go to other Chinese churches nor even to any Anglo church. Eighty percent of the ABC hope to attend a church where English is the primary language. They are not satisfied with the OBC-led churches; however, they do not feel fully adapted to an Anglo church. They feel that they are a second-class group. This is our behind-the-scenes struggle as we focus on outreach and evangelism to Chinese Americans.

The fourth difficulty is the great mobility of the Chinese congregational population. Members of the Chinese churches include international students, professionals, intellectuals, as well as blue-collar laborers and restaurant workers. International students move every two to three years. Professionals and intellectuals are not very stable because of frequent job relocation. One statistic cited at the St. Louis Chinese Church Council in June 2005 claims that about 60 percent of the baptized members for the last five years in a big local Chinese church have left due to the factors of job relocation, further study, or a return to their place of birth. In the last three years, LOC baptized twenty-four adults and nine children,

---

[3] Helen Lee, "Silent Exodus," *Christianity Today* (August 12, 1996): 50.

[4] Lee, "Silent Exodus," 52.

yet 40 percent left for the same reasons. Transience, therefore, is an obstacle to training leadership for the purpose of outreach and evangelism.

Chinese Cultures and Worldview

Overseas-born Chinese still live with a strong sense of Chinese culture and the traditional Chinese worldview. Even though the American-born Chinese are more westernized, they retain some traditional concepts, and those concepts continue from generation to generation. For example, Chinese children traditionally think that they have obligations to take care of their parents. No matter how much they breathe in the western ideal of individualism, they have greater struggles than do Anglo-American kids in this matter. The concept of filial piety is rooted deeply in their minds; it is part of being Chinese. They believe that it is appropriate to follow this.

Some Chinese Americans still think that the increase of missionary activity coincided with gunboat policy and colonial expansion of the Western powers and was influenced by them. They think Christianity is a Western religion, which is in contradistinction to the indigenous religions such as Confucianism, Taoism, and folk religions. Even worse, some still think that one more Christian conversion means one less Chinese person exists.[5] Thankfully, the majority of the Chinese Americans no longer buy into this misunderstanding.

To share the Gospel with the Chinese Americans, we need first to seek to understand their worldview and values. Chinese language is the Asian equivalent of Latin, and Chinese culture is the mother of many Asian cultures. The Chinese culture indirectly and directly gave birth to other Asian cultures, such as Korean, Japanese, and Vietnamese culture. The more we understand the Chinese culture, the better we can share the Gospel with traditional Chinese people. In fact, Chinese culture does not necessarily contradict the Christian faith. Nor do we need to water down our faith to win Chinese souls. We need to find some similar concepts as entry points. We need to pray for our target group and let God work in their hearts; then we will see God's guidance in the ministry of our outreach and evangelism. As we share the Gospel with Chinese Americans at LOC, we have encountered the following worldviews and concepts.

---

[5] Enoch Wan, "Christianity in the Eye of Traditional Chinese," *Chinese around the World* (July 1999).

First, Chinese culture lacks the concept of transcendence. The mainstream philosophy in the Chinese culture is Confucianism. Because of its influence, the traditional Chinese emphasize their horizontal relationships with others and pay less attention to the vertical relationship with God. Although evidences show that Chinese philosophy had a concept of "heaven" in the beginning, it failed to develop this idea in following generations. The Western culture, under the influence of the Greek philosophy, emphasizes metaphysics. The word *philosophy* literally means to "love wisdom." Yet this understanding is different from the Chinese culture. To the Chinese, philosophy means to know how to be a genuine man or sage, a wise man with good and noble attributes, one who knows how the world operates (naturally, socially, politically, etc.) and which choice to make in any given human circumstance. The central theme of Confucianism is the "art of living." It does not care much about how man has come into existence, but instead focuses on how man by himself can live in harmony with nature and with others in community.[6] This is an ultimate goal of Chinese philosophy. Chinese culture is also rooted in the experience of suffering. This is why Chinese welcome the concept of nothingness in Taoism and the concept of emptiness and suffering in Buddhism. The Chinese culture's understanding of suffering is formed by the lost harmony with nature and other people. Finally, Chinese people emphasize cosmic harmony, but they focus on the existential experience of "harmony," rather than the ontological meaning of the "cosmic."

Second, Chinese culture is predominantly a system of ethical realism. Ethical consciousness applies to five different primary relationships: husband to wife, parents to children, older brother to younger brother, king and noble to populace, and friend to friend. All ideas can be summed up in one word, namely, *jen* (humanity). This is the central idea in the Confucian system. The word *jen* involves the realization of the self and the creation of a social order. The sage is a person who is living "humanity" out in his life, including earnestness, broadness, truthfulness, diligence, and generosity. Chinese are seeking ethical perfection.

Third, Chinese culture lacks the concept of sin. Due to the influence of Confucianism, Chinese culture does not confess the evil nature of human

---

[6] Andy Chow, "Sharing the Gospel to the Traditional Chinese," *Chinese around the World* (September 1998).

beings. Chinese believe that society can improve through education. To confess having sins is to be weak. The whole ethical system is focused on self-effort and self-power. One should not ask another power to help. Therefore facing the reality of sin, one may either reject it, or hide, or pretend to be good. Yet the popular way is to compare one's behavior with others and judge others if they are doing worse. This is the way Chinese distract themselves from guilt.

Fourth, Chinese culture lacks an eschatological future. In the *Analects*, the classic Confucian writings, it is said that someone asked Confucius about death and the world after death. He replied, "How could I know if I cannot fully understand the art of living?" Traditional Chinese culture seldom talks about the world after death. However, Chinese culture borrowed from Buddhism and Hinduism the concept of an eschatological future. It appears in the concepts of transmigration, hell, and so on. Being pragmatists, Chinese sages may be both faithful Confucians and devoted Buddhists, just to cover the bases. Chinese are really in need of knowing the truth.

Fifth, Chinese culture emphasizes the teaching of filial piety. What does filial piety mean? Technically speaking, this concept focuses on devotion to one's parents. In reality, it translates into love and respect for parents, just like the Fourth Commandment: "Honor your father and mother" (Exodus 20:12). Traditionally, Chinese philosophers emphasized the teaching of filial piety as the fountain of all good conduct. From genuine and comprehensive love toward one's own parents, one may naturally learn to be benevolent to all living creatures; to be affectionate toward mankind as a whole; to be loyal to his country and its rulers; to perform the duties of a free citizen; to be faithful in keeping obligations; to be righteous in action; and to behave peacefully and act justly in all dealings. That is why the classics of filial piety say, "It is filial piety which forms the root of all virtues, and with it all enlightening studies come into existence."

Sixth, Chinese culture's emphasis on practicality has created religious syncretism. Although the Chinese practice various religions, such as Buddhism, Confucianism, Taoism, and folk religions, all those religions merely give spiritual exercises and religious guidance for self-help. If one can follow the instructions and practice them faithfully, he will enter the highest spirituality. Chinese culture does not want to exclude any religion; therefore people welcome religious pluralism. Folk religions even create more deities for two purposes: (a) to give the people a sense of protection and (b) to give them different exercises to achieve the spiritual heights, based on personal preference. From the Lutheran perspective, Chinese culture promotes different kinds of legalism.

Strategies

Since the LOC has not worked with the international students very much, the following suggestions are focused on the ways to share the Gospel with traditional Chinese, Chinese intellectuals, restaurant workers, and American-born Chinese. I also share the outreach plan used at LOC. Finally, I list some materials that LOC is using for outreach and evangelism.

To share the Gospel with traditional Chinese. An outreach ministry commited to sharing the Gospel with traditional Chinese needs to have patience. Do not try to win them by debate because you are not persuading a person about an idea, but rather touching on his or her very essence as a Chinese person. Without being enlightened by the Holy Spirit, one cannot be released from the deeply rooted Chinese culture and boldly seek the truth. Be ready to share the faith with them at any time. As the Scripture says, "[B]ut in your hearts regard Christ the Lord as holy, always being prepared to make a defense to anyone who asks you for a reason for the hope that is in you; yet do it with gentleness and respect" (1 Peter 3:15–16). Try to find out if there is any similarity between the Scriptures and the Chinese culture for outreach and evangelism.

The first overlap between Scripture and Chinese culture can be found in the concept of transcendence, which goes back to the very beginning of Chinese history. The connection is in the practical expression of the sacred within Christianity. The concept of transcendence need not develop into abstract thinking as we see in Greek philosophy. Hebrew culture has the concept of transcendence, but they express their understanding of God in a practical way. In the Old Testament, the Hebrews believed in God the Creator who is almighty God, but they expressed their faith in a concrete way. The Book of Proverbs is an example of how they express their faith and offer spiritual instruction to adherents. Their faith was actively expressed in their life. Through divine action, God restored the vertical relationship which man had broken, and based on that reconciliation men and women could reestablish healthy relationships with one another on the horizontal level. In the New Testament, Jesus expressed the truth in practical terms, as well. He said, "I am the way, and the truth, and the life. No one comes to the Father except through Me" (John 14:6). By the grace of Jesus Christ, cosmic harmony is restored with God, with nature, and with fellow human beings. The Christian life is not merely a truth for the present life. It is the truth of all eternity.

Another link between the Bible and Chinese culture is the theme of suffering. Ancient Israelites understood their faith as the solution to suffering. In the Exodus event, God freed the Hebrew nation from suffering and bondage in Egypt when they cried out to God. The Exodus experience can help link the suffering of the Chinese with the Christian faith.

We must remember that the Word of God is not an abstract idea and theory at all. The Reformation motto "Scripture Alone" is to challenge people to forsake the dead and lifeless philosophy and turn to seek truth of life in the Bible. If we faithfully preach the Word and Sacraments, traditional Chinese will finally find how the Word of God is so relevant to their lives. The Word of God continually guides every adherent to walk in His path.

Second, we can also link the Ten Commandments to the concept of filial piety. In Chinese culture, filial piety is the root of all virtues. It is the reason for ethical and moral order. Through filial piety, the society and family are tied closely together. Government officials function as the parents of the people. The earth is the mother of all aspects of nature. In the Bible, the Fourth Commandment also emphasizes honoring the father and mother. In Luther's Small Catechism, Luther uses the same approach to expand the commandment in a broader sense. This commandment is not limited to a family setting. Luther says, "We should fear and love God so that we do not despise or anger our parents and other authorities, but honor them, serve and obey them, love and cherish them."[7] Luther's words can be explained as follows: "Parents are fathers, mothers, and guardians; other authorities are all those whom God has placed over us at home, in government, at school, at the place where we work, and in the church."[8] The theme of the Ten Commandments is to remember the source and root of our creation, that is, from God and through our parents. If we respect God and our parents, we will learn to respect the lives of others,

---

[7] *Luther's Small Catechism with Explanation* (St. Louis: Concordia, 1986, 1991), 12.

[8] *Luther's Small Catechism with Explanation*, 74.

their property, their reputation, and so forth. Furthermore, as we deal with the issue of ancestor worship, we may distinguish practices based on filial piety from fear of animistic spirits or the desire to get protection and good things from the ancestors' power. This distinction would avoid miscommunication.

Third, we must be careful how we share with the traditional Chinese about sin. We must avoid getting into a hot debate between sinful nature and acts of sin. Some say, "Chinese culture looks at sin as sinful deeds, but Christian theology conceives of sinful nature." That tack is a losing proposition with respect to sharing about sin with the Chinese Americans. The Bible defines sin as "missing the point" or "not achieving the standard." The definition of sin rests on God's standard. Because the defintion of sin and the standard by which our activities are judged comes from God, there is no debate about what is sin. Instead, whatever is not up to God's standard is sin. For example, "If you know the standard of greed and you break it, you are a sinner" or "If you know something should not be done but have done it, you sin." The seventh chapter of Romans does not merely describe the destructiveness of the sinful nature in Paul's struggle, but also the sinful acts he has done. This approach can help a traditional Chinese to understand their sins.

Fourth, as we share with the traditional Chinese about the ethical system and social orders, we should first appreciate their search for beauty and goodness. There are some similarities between *jen* (humanity) and biblical love, such as selflessness and the goal of blessing others. Yet the difference between *jen* and godly love is in motivation. For traditional Chinese, a person creates within himself or herself the ethical motivation to achieve perfection. However, if the action does not achieve what a person expects and desires, he or she will be disappointed. If you fail, then you will likely not repeat that action. Ever since the influx of Buddhism in Chinese culture, the expression of *jen* has been linked to religious works or merit. As a result, the exercise of *jen* as works can help one achieve spiritual heights. In that way, the action of *jen* shifts from being a selfless ideal to a selfish desire.

Christianity separates the action of love (*jen*) from the path of salvation. Christian faith is about how God loves the world and gave His only begotten Son, Jesus Christ, to die for us and freely offered us such wonderful grace. Then, we respond to the love of God by loving our neighbor with a thankful heart and serving everyone in our community. Christianity is a Gospel religion and not another one of the law religions. Martin Luther states in a treatise "On Christian Liberty," "A Christian is a perfectly free lord of all, subject to none. A Christian is a perfectly dutiful servant of all, subject to all."[9]

Finally, Christians can use the concept of vocation to engage Chinese in a dialogue about Chinese ethical consciousness and the five ethical relationships. The concept of vocation challenges a Christian to build a harmonious relationship with others to bring forth a harmonious society. In the Christian concept of vocation, God calls us to fulfill different roles in a society so that God blesses the world through us. A Christian can be a father, an officer, a husband, a leader at the church, a son, and many more things. The idea of vocation reminds us to take seriously our obligations and seek to fulfill our roles with a joyful attitude. Finally, this idea helps traditional Chinese see that the Bible is practical for our daily life, our family, and our nation.

To share the Gospel with the Chinese intellectuals. Professionals and intellectuals are those who have completed college and graduate study. Many Chinese professionals and intellectuals are working in scientific research fields. In mainland China, only 3 percent of the Chinese population are intellectuals. To share the Gospel with them, we should pay attention to their cultural background and worldview (as mentioned above). We also need to understand any other difficulties preventing them from accepting Christianity. A survey asked two groups of Chinese intellectuals, from Taiwan and China, about the difficulties in hearing the Gospel. More than 60 percent of the intellectuals from mainland China said the first and greatest obstacle is the conflict between science and religion.[10] Others related to this conflict are the believability of the miracles and Jesus' resurrection. Thirty percent of the Taiwanese intellectuals agree. For them, however, this conflict ranks second in making Christianity difficult to accept. Some churches try to prove God with reason. They attract these intellectuals quickly. Yet later,

---

[9] Luther, "On Christianity Liberty," in *Luther's Works*, vol. 31 (Philadelphia: Muhlenberg, 1957), 344.

[10] Tsu-Kung Chuang, *Ripening Harvest: A Mission Strategy for Mainland Chinese Intellectuals in North America* (Paradise, PA: Ambassadors for Christ, 1995), Table 19.

as Chinese intellectuals face other issues that their reason cannot account for, they leave the church. In the past, many Chinese churches would talk about how many Chinese intellectuals became Christians yet omit that there were many who left the church, as well. Our church emphasizes that faith does not merely require knowledge about God but also belief in Jesus. We have to confess Him as Savior and confess our sins. We have to trust Baptism as the means of grace and trust the Bible as the Word of God, which is beyond our reason to imagine and explain. The greatest thing to share with Chinese intellectuals is not theology, but Christology. They need a systematic understanding of the theology of the cross. Then the roots of their Christian life will grow deeply in Christ.

Two other great difficulties for these two groups of Chinese intellectuals in accepting Christianity are being too busy and the bad behavior of some Christians in churches. As we all know, actions speak louder than words. On the other hand, many Chinese intellectuals truly appreciate the love of Christians and their kindness. In fact, many of the Chinese intellectuals who took the survey are OBC, and they have gone through steps for settling down in the United States. Many of them were postdoctorate and international students in universities in the beginning. These new immigrants or new students faced many difficulties in cultural adaptation. The LOC, as other Chinese churches, has devoted much effort to helping these newcomers to the United States, such as helping them with host families, providing them with English-as-second-language classes, teaching them to drive, and donating furniture and other items to them. The love of Christians with whom they come into contact has drawn these Chinese intellectuals to consider the Christian faith.

In addition, Chinese intellectuals are generally fond of reading. They have strong reading ability and high comprehension. They like thinking for themselves and dislike people pushing them to accept any religion. Therefore our church applied for a grant to set up a resource center. We bought many Chinese Christian books for them to check out. The response has been very good.

Finally, to share the Gospel with these Chinese intellectuals, we may need to publish more testimonies and stories about how Chinese intellectuals became Christians. To produce these testimonies has two advantages. First, such stories highlight that many Chinese intellectuals have become Christians. Although one believes in God and believes in the biblical account through faith, not reason, science is not really in conflict with religion. Christians are not intellectual or cultural lightweights. In fact, many Christians are well-read, thoughtful, and culturally informed. In the past 300 years, 92 percent of the outstanding scientists in the world believed in God and most of them were devout Christians. Such testimonies would help Chinese intellectuals leave behind their pride and be receptive to a Christian witness about God. Then through the power of the Holy Spirit, they may come to a knowledge of the truth. The second advantage of published testimonies is to reduce the level of intellectual debate so that we may go into the core of the Gospel, Jesus Christ.

To share the Gospel with the restaurant workers. The Chinese church in the United States has lost sight of restaurant workers. As a group, they simply fall off the radar screen of most churches, for various reasons. First, they work long hours without a break on Sunday, which prevents them from coming to our general church activities and ministries. Second, they know little English and are hard to assimilate to the American culture. They have little formal education and earn a living through hard labor. As a rule, this group only associates within a small circle of people, such as their friends and family members. Restaurant workers are known for their habit of gambling, even to the extent of becoming addicted to it.

Rather than following the more intellectually appealing or socially rewarding religions of China, restaurant workers tend to practice folk religion and ancestor worship. They are superstitious and seek protection and blessing from their ancestors and spirits. Since they have minimal contact with churches, they associate church with the middle class and intellectuals,[11] or view it as merely a social gathering for those who are emotionally weak.[12]

A church worker who ministers to this group has said, "The restaurant workers have low social status. They feel inferiority and self-pity as compared with others. They think they are quite unlucky in their fate. If it

---

[11] It is not surprising because, in the 1980s and 1990s, many Chinese churches began as a Bible study group on college campuses. Due to the time and education gap, the restaurant workers cannot partake.

[12] "Reach the Heart of Restaurant Workers with the Gospel" *Chinese around the World.*

were not for their next children, they would rather want to go back to their home country. They refuse to say they have sin.[13]

To share the Gospel with restaurant workers, we need to be more flexible with our schedules. Instead of hoping restaurant workers will show up at the church for worship on a Sunday morning, it is best to arrange a small group or fellowship that meets somewhere else, at some other time of day (or night), and on a different day of the week. A few years ago, we arranged a late-night Bible study group during the week for these people and organized special programs late Sunday night for them. These programs generated a good response, as indicated by the number of people who attended. So we learned that these people would come to church, or meet elsewhere, if we could find a time that did not conflict with their work schedule. Sometimes they enjoyed being at the Bible study group and did not leave until 1:00 or 2:00 a.m. We were also encouraged by the fact that they often willingly brought new friends to our Bible study group.

Due to their fear of the American culture and environment, they would carefully protect themselves. They do not want to be cheated and to be disappointed. It takes time and church members must be patient in their efforts to build a warm relationship with them. We must not push them to respond to the Gospel. In our church, some restaurant workers have been in touch with us for a few years. In that time, their feelings about the church have changed from enmity to friendship.

Through sharing the Gospel, we let the restaurant workers know that God loves us. No matter who we are, or where or when we have to work, He accepts us. We are very precious in the eyes of God. Besides forgiveness, the Gospel also helps build their self-esteem. Finally, the English as second language class and citizenship class meet their practical needs in adapting to the United States and let them know that God can reveal His love and grace in the spiritual realm, as well as in their daily life.

To share the Gospel with the American-born Chinese (ABC). Superficially, there is no more difference sharing the Gospel to the American-born Chinese than with a Caucasian or an African American. However, ABC are unique even though sharing the English language. Although ABC are easier to assimilate to mainstream American culture, they may not

---

[13] "Reach the Heart of Restaurant Workers with the Gospel" *Chinese around the World.*

completely feel comfortable in an Anglo church. These ABC want their parents to understand their unique needs and have better communication with them. Some OBC parents have trouble communicating with their ABC children because of the limited ability they possess to speak English. The generation gap is a common issue between ABC and OBC in many Chinese American families. In a church, ABC may prefer a completely different form of worship.

To reach out to the ABC is not merely a matter of strategy but also relates to church structure. Helping ABC overcome their struggles and become a core group of the church is important. We have to trust them and give them our blessing to try new ideas for the needs of their peer group. We should include ABC in the leadership team and share the responsibility with them of fulfilling the Great Commission. As a whole, it is important to train ABC and to let ABC engage in outreach and evangelism to their peer group. Although the American-born Chinese people at LOC are still young and few in numbers, we have started giving them responsibility. For example, they help as big brothers or big sisters to keep the classrooms clean and all their classmates behaving well.

To share the Gospel with an effective outreach plan (Light of Christ model). In order to share the Gospel with Chinese Americans, we need to create an effective outreach plan and implement it with perseverance. In our church, we have tried different outreach strategies, such as weekly ESL class, weekly visitation and personal evangelism, a Chinese resource center, host family caring groups, monthly Cantonese fellowship, home Bible study groups, a weekly luncheon after the Sunday service, and more. In the beginning of the church, we organized an activity once every month, which we called "fishing-pool activity." The purpose was to establish a network and build friendships. Chinese Americans are relational and communal. Many of them came from Asia, leaving behind their communities, relatives, and support network. They and their immediate family (wives and children) came to the United States to start a new life. Especially when there was a Chinese festival, they may have felt lonely and homesick. Fishing-pool activities are opportunities for us to contact them and show our love to them, while also giving us a good excuse to call them and invite them to other ministries, for example, Bible study group and Sunday worship. A newsletter named *Gospel Bridge* is published every quarter to strengthen communication with our target group, congregation members, and even with those who financially support our ministry.

Material used for the purpose of outreach and evangelism. Appropriate outreach materials are crucial for effective outreach and evangelism. At LOC, we chose different kinds of cassette tapes, booklets, and Gospel tracts to give to our target group. We give every new visitor a package of these materials when one comes to our worship service. To make sure we are communicating clearly with Chinese Americans, we always seek material that has both English and Chinese versions, or is bilingual. For example, Luther's Small Catechism and Explanation have three different versions— English, traditional Chinese characters, and simplified characters—for a Chinese church to use. We publish *Good News Magazine* in three language versions to enrich the lives of Chinese Christians with quality Christian writing. Lutheran Hour Ministry has booklets with two language versions. Their cassette tapes and Gospel tracts are also very useful. In addition, they offer the Chinese Bible in video form for outreach and evangelism to the Chinese. Occasionally, LOC will prepare some promotional products, such as mugs, key chains, and more to give the new visitors as a token of love. We will also prepare promotional materials such as brochures for them to learn about LOC.

CONCLUSION

Outreach and evangelism to Chinese Americans in the United States is a stepping-stone for world mission and global Chinese mission. Therefore we need to invest more effort and gather all the resources together to achieve this goal and fulfill the command of our Lord in the Great Commission. Financial support, prayer, and teamwork are important for the success of this ministry. May God bless the ministry at LOC. May God also bless the Chinese ministry elsewhere in the United States.

African Immigrants: Models for Effective Outreach Ministry

Yohannes Mengsteab
National Director, New Mission Fields Development,
The Lutheran Church—Missouri Synod

The purpose of this paper is to present a ministry model that has proven effective in outreach ministry to African immigrants in the United States of America. Before discussing the ministry model however, it is important, first of all, to define what the phrase "African immigrants" means.

By African immigrants I mean individuals born in Africa who have entered the United States voluntarily, and not through slave trade of earlier centuries. In other words, present-day African immigrants are latecomers into the American scene, beginning their arrival in the mid-twentieth century and growing in numbers in the last two decades.

African immigrants can be classified into three groups: (1) those who came as students and tourists, (2) those who came as businessmen and women, (3) and those who came as refugees and recently through lottery visas. The first two groups and those who came through lottery visas have left their countries of origin voluntarily and can be classified as immigrants. Refugees, however, have left their countries of origin because of political and/or religious persecutions; they entered the United States voluntarily, but they left their countries of origin against their will.

One important characteristic common to all three groups is that African immigrants are for the most part risk-takers, leaders, and creative people within their countries of origin. They have brought economic vitality to their communities in the United States, as they had in their countries of origin. Martin Franzier has indicated that, while the

United States government sends $1 billion a year in aid to all African nations, the approximately two million African immigrants in the United States are sending $3 billion a year to their countries of origin.[1]

Even though the African immigrants tend to assimilate into the American culture faster than other recent immigrant groups, most of them still maintain their unique cultural identities. While some of them, such as the Nigerians, Ethiopians, Eritreans, Ghanaians, South Africans, and Egyptians, are doing well economically and socially, the newest groups, such as the Sudanese, Liberians, and Somali Bantus, are economically and/or culturally challenged.[2] However, even in the groups that are doing well economically and socially, there is a greater proportion of underemployment than in the mainstream. Many African immigrants hold two jobs to support their families in the United States adequately and to provide for their extended family members in Africa.

Cultural Background

Despite what some people may think, Africa does not have a single culture. If language is one of the indicators of cultural groupings, there are thousands of African languages and dialects, thus thousands of different cultures. A country of four million people, such as Eritrea, for example, has nine language groups, thus nine different cultures.

However, there are some similarities in the African immigrants' cultural backgrounds. These cultural similarities may also be common in other third-world countries, but the commonality in the African immigrant communities is manifested in the growing interest of the African immigrants to band together.[3] For the purpose of outreach ministry to African immigrants, we will consider three major similarities: communications style, family values, and religious fervor.

1. *Communications Style.* Even though they might be educated in Western educational institutions, for most African immigrants the default mode of communication is oral. They grew up in communities where history is preserved orally, in which grandparents and

---

[1] Martin Frazier, "African American and African Immigrants," *People's Weekly World Newspaper* (May 19, 2005).

[2] Frazier, "African American and African Immigrants."

[3] Frazier, "African American and African Immigrants."

parents tell their children and grandchildren the stories of the community with the hope that they will also tell the tradition to their children.

2. **Family Values.** For all of the African immigrants, with the exception of those who come from dysfunctional families, family includes grandparents, uncles and aunts, cousins, and distant relatives. In small immigrant communities, the family may also include the tribe. Families are also, for the most part, male dominated, and the elderly are given positions of leadership in the family, as well as the community.[4]

3. **Religious Fervor.** Africans are very religious people. Religion is part of their psyche. And the so-called "excluded middle" identified by Hiebert and Meneses in Western culture is not excluded in the African culture.[5] African immigrants are mostly Christians, Muslims, and a few animists. Even though many may be disconnected from the church or the mosque because they are in a new land and adjusting to new cultural systems, the majority of the African immigrants believes in God.

Finally, African immigrants, like many refugees and immigrants in the United States, long to go back to their countries of origin. Their longing to go back to their countries of origin is manifested in that many of them send the remains of the deceased back to Africa, as well as that they remain actively involved in the politics and the economic developments of their countries of origin.[6]

Economic Power

As indicated earlier, African immigrants in North America are among the most risk-taking and leadership types of their countrymen.[7] Their immigration to the United States has resulted in the so-called "Brain Drain" of

---

[4] Paul G. Hiebert and Eloise Hiebert Meneses, *Incarnational Ministry: Planting Churches in Band, Tribal, Peasant, and Urban Societies* (Grand Rapids: Baker, 1995), 91ff.

[5] Hiebert and Meneses, *Incarnational Ministry*, 91ff. The "excluded middle" is the spiritual world in which good and evil spirits reign.

[6] Frazier, "African American and African Immigrants."

[7] Frazier, "African American and African Immigrants."

Africa, in which the most educated and entrepreneurial members of the society are leaving Africa for stronger economies.

As Frazier and many other observers would concur, African immigrants are making significant economic contributions to America. Besides the highly educated and highly paid professionals and businessmen and women, thousands of African taxi drivers and laborers populate all major metropolitan areas providing much-needed services.[8]

African Immigrant Ministry
LCMS—Historical Account

Even though the African immigrants started coming to the United States in the 1960s, The Lutheran Church—Missouri Synod did not start working with them until two decades later, in the late 1980s. The first LCMS work among African immigrants was to Eritrean immigrants in Philadelphia, Pennsylvania, started in 1989, and at St. John's Lutheran Church in Toronto, Ontario, in 1990.

Work among Sudanese immigrants by Trinity Lutheran Church in Des Moines, Iowa, began in 1992. Through Lutheran Child and Family Services of Des Moines, Trinity Lutheran Church sponsored a Sudanese family, and through the leadership of the first refugee family a congregation of three hundred Sudanese was established. The congregation in Des Moines became the mother of the more than twenty Sudanese ministries started since 1995 throughout North America.

The African Immigrant Ministry in the northeastern region of the United States started in 1995. A congregation of Liberian immigrants joined the LCMS and started seven more congregations in New York, New Jersey, Pennsylvania, and Connecticut. The work with the Ethiopian and Eritrean immigrants in Washington, DC also started in 1995.

Through the leadership of the Board for Mission Services, North American Missions, the African Immigrant Ministry (AIM) Task Force was organized on February 9, 1996. Since the organization of the AIM Task Force, more than eighty congregations and ministries serving African immigrants were started by the end of 2004.[9]

---

[8] Frazier, "African American and African Immigrants."

[9] African Immigrant Ministry Task Force of The Lutheran Church—Missouri Synod, meeting minutes 1996–2005.

Moreover, in 1995, only one active African immigrant pastor of the LCMS was serving African immigrants. In 2005 there are more than ten pastors and more than fifty people in training to assume pastoral leadership in those congregations and ministries that have started since 1996.

This phenomenal success happened because of the Lord's guidance and the power of the Holy Spirit. However, guided by the Holy Spirit, there were some strategic decisions that propelled AIM into a growing mission movement in North America. The African immigrant leaders realized that they are in a mission field and approaches to African immigrant missions in North America should not assume a churched culture, but a mission field that takes into account the raising of responsible leaders for a young church. The mission strategy that was developed by the African Immigrant Task Force in 1996 was based on the need of an emerging mission field and was to become the blueprint for the last nine years.

Ministry Goals and Objectives

The ministry goals and objectives of AIM are summarized in its vision statement from 2000: "In partnership with LCMS Districts, we will have missionary congregations, which have a passion for the lost, serving the Lord of life with African immigrants in every city and village in North America, where African immigrants live." This mission vision was implemented with ministry values that the African immigrant leaders held as important, which are in addition to the core values of North America Missions:

a. We are Lutheran Christians who understand that we are part of the Universal Church. We adhere to the Lutheran Confessions in our teaching and practice for we believe that they are true expositions of the Scriptures.

b. We are a missionary organization. We will concentrate on planting new mission stations so that there be a Christian presence in every city and village where African immigrants live in North America.

c. We are African immigrants. We recognize that African immigrants have special needs and we will work hard to address those special needs as God enables us.

d. We believe that God gives all the gifts necessary for His Church so that His people will be guided and equipped for mission and ministry. We therefore will empower lay leaders to lead their people in ministry and will provide for them needed leadership development programs.[10]

As one may be able to surmise, AIM strategy revolved around leadership development and church planting, keeping in mind the doctrine of the priesthood of all believers (1 Peter 2:9). This strategy led to the establishment of the Ethnic Immigrant Institute of Theology of Concordia Seminary, St. Louis, which started its ministry in 2002 to train those lay leaders engaged in the start of the more than eighty congregations and ministries since 1996.

In order to accomplish the ministry vision set in 1996, AIM established five goals:

1. Recruit and place 10 missionaries in the major metropolitan areas by the end of 2002;

2. Identify and train 100 leaders by the end of 2005;

3. Develop and implement leadership development programs in all those metropolitan areas where missionaries are placed by September of 2002;

4. Develop ways to raise funds and other resource materials for AIM mission starts and leadership development programs by September of 2001; and

5. Work toward increased cooperation with the Board for Black Ministry.[11]

The African Immigrant Ministry Task Force has accomplished most of the goals and objectives that were set in 1996; this is a testimony to the strength of the ministry techniques that were employed to accomplish the goals.

CHIEF OUTREACH MINISTRY TECHNIQUES

Several ministry techniques have served AIM well, based on those five goals. These include partnerships, intentional leadership identification and development, and the use of natural networks for the purpose of church planting and outreach ministry.

[10] AIM-LCMS Strategic Statement, 3ff.

[11] AIM-LCMS Strategic Statement 2000 edition, 3–4.

Partnerships

AIM leaders of the LCMS realized, early on, that starting mission work in the African immigrant communities in the traditional way is slow and too little too late. The traditional church-planting strategy in the LCMS, according to Dr. Robert Scudieri, Associate Director for North American Mission, is that (a) districts do mission planting, (b) closely tied to land acquisitions, and (c) have to have a full-time seminary graduate for a mission planter.

Recognizing the challenges of the traditional church-planting methods, AIM leaders decided to work through partners to overcome the challenges of a new mission field. Working through districts in partnerships with local congregations, ministries to African immigrants were to start throughout North America. Since most of these programs started as side-by-side ministries of existing urban congregations, they are also able to revitalize urban congregations that were in a precipitous decline. Without doubt, they gave some urban congregations a new lease on life.

Moreover, the partnership of these ministries with host or mother congregations freed African immigrants from having to shoulder the burden of buying and maintaining a building. The experience of the mother congregations also gave the African immigrant congregations stability, as well as doctrinal guidance to be fully incorporated into the ministerium of the LCMS.

Intentional Leadership Identification and Development

One of the most crucial facts that the African immigrant leaders identified in 1996 was that North America is a mission field. A mission work in a new mission field does not assume that there are or will be pastors who come to provide pastoral leadership for the growing ministry needs. Leaders are intentionally identified from a group that a missionary gathers, and leaders are trained to take leadership positions. Some of the African immigrants have experienced a mission setting where the missionaries have taken pastoral leadership roles and delayed the identification and training of local leaders, thus stifling the growth of a national church. On the contrary, the missionaries who were timely in identifying, training, and handing on responsibilities to natives have witnessed the rapid growth of national churches. Mekane Yesus Evangelical Church of Ethiopia, which within half a century grew from half a million to more than four million members, is a prime example of missionary practice that allowed for the development of local leaders. The African immigrant leaders of the LCMS, having known the mission strategy of churches like Mekane Yesus Evangelical Church of Ethiopia, decided to adopt leadership development as a strategy for the church-planting movement in the North American scene.

The strategy was to deploy ten African immigrant missionaries in strategic metropolitan areas and ethnic communities with a mandate to identify ten leaders each and supervise the planting of ten congregations. Seven missionaries were deployed in 2002, and there were more than seventy LCMS congregations in ministry to African immigrants; the growth was phenomenal and proved the strategy to be sound.

The success of the strategy of church planting through leadership development necessitated the development of a distance theological education program. This program leads to ordination while training the church planters without removing them from their contexts. The Ethnic Immigrant Institute of Theology (EIIT) was organized in 2002 primarily to train the African immigrant leaders. The ministry of EIIT has expanded since and is serving all ethnic immigrant ministries of the LCMS.

AIM lifted up the position of the missionary to its rightful place. The missionary in AIM does not plant the churches, but identifies, trains, and supports leaders to do so. However, since one of the core values of AIM leadership is faithfulness to the Lutheran Confessions, sound theological education for the church planters became important. Thus the partnership of AIM with Concordia Seminary, St. Louis, was not and is not optional, but rather is a necessity.

The challenge of the LCMS congregations engaged in cross-cultural ministry is also exacerbated by the lack of seminary-trained LCMS ethnic pastors. Because LCMS church-planting strategy mainly depends on residential seminary-trained pastors, most congregations in changing communities could not intentionally raise and develop missionaries from the new immigrant communities. In essence, no seminarians came from African immigrant backgrounds, so no pastors with immigrant heritage could be sent to immigrant congregations. What AIM did for these congregations in changing neighborhoods was help open their eyes to leaders in the community for church planting and evangelistic ministries.

Natural Networks for the Purpose of Church Planting and Outreach Ministry

Urban missiologists, such as Harvie Conn and Manuel Ortiz, have recognized the power of social networks in cities. Conn and Ortiz point out that cities are "holistic system[s] of networks" through which communities form. These networks encompass geography, social constructs, institutions, political systems, culture, and religion.[12] The networks that are based on ethnic and cultural backgrounds are what are referred to as natural networks for the purpose of this paper. These natural networks may also take political, religious, or geographical forms. In the case of the African immigrants, they are not geographically concentrated, and the congregations that are planted tend to be regional congregations that attract people based on natural networks.

Consequently, the African immigrant congregations and ministries of the LCMS are classified into two groups: English-speaking and language-specific congregations. The English-speaking congregations, such as St. Augustine Lutheran Church of Fort Wayne, Indiana, tend to be pan-African congregations. St. Augustine membership includes more than a dozen ethnic and national groups. However the English-speaking congregations in most cases are dominated by the nationality and/or the ethnic background of the pastor leader. For example, the members of Christ Assembly Lutheran Church of Staten Island, New York, and Philadelphia, which are led by Liberian leaders, are predominantly Liberian immigrants.

The majority of the African immigrant congregations are, however, language-specific congregations: Oromifa and Amharic speaking congregations for Ethiopians, Tigrigna speaking for Eritreans, Nuer speaking for Sudanese, and so forth. These congregations are now challenged with the second-generation members of their communities, for whom English is their first language. Congregations, such as the Eritrean Evangelical Lutheran Church of Downey, California, are having English sermons for the second generation during the language-specific worship services.

As long as new immigrants continue to come from the countries of the congregation of first-generation immigrants, there will be a need for language-specific services. However, the challenge of reaching to the second

---

[12] Harvie Conn and Manuel Ortiz, *Urban Ministry: The Kingdom, the City, and the People of God* (Downers Grove, IL: InterVarsity, 2001), 24.

generation is pressuring these congregations to become English-speaking or bilingual congregations.

Nonetheless, the main factor for attracting African immigrants to these congregations is the natural networks of their members. They are able to invite friends and relatives, countrymen, and people who come from their continent because of their cultural and tribal affinities. This validates the complex networks of city systems, which Harvie Conn, Manuel Ortiz, Paul Hiebert, and other urban missiologists have recognized. Even though the African immigrants have left behind their countries of origin, their villages and cities, including their extended families, they do not totally isolate themselves from their communities; consequently, their networks extend even beyond the cities in which they live. Thus the ability of the immigrant to network is a tremendous asset for mission and evangelism.

CONCLUSION

AIM has prospered in the last decade of the twentieth century because of the power of the Holy Spirit. Moreover, the Spirit of God has assembled leaders at the right time and the right place to provide a missionary leadership to a growing mission field. The leadership of AIM has the ability to understand cultural diversity and has the sensitivity to work effectively across cultures.

Because of the cultural diversity of the African immigrant communities in North America, the leadership of AIM has focused on leadership development as a strategy to reach out to the various ethnic and national groups. This approach gave the leadership of AIM the ability and flexibility to target individual ethnic and national communities with clear focus. And its continued growth will be influenced by how the system of the LCMS is able to give room to its strategy and the talents of its growing leadership circle.

HAITIANS:
A NEW MILLENNIUM MISSION FIELD

S. T. Williams Jr.
(Assisted by Marky Klessa)
Pastor, St. Paul Lutheran Church, Los Angeles, California
(Formerly with LCMS National Missions, Lincoln, Nebraska)

CHURCH PLANTING, MISSION OUTPOST, EVANGELISTIC OUTREACH

The biblical formation of developing a church-planting movement has led the Lutheran Church to become one of the fastest growing evangelistic outreaching church bodies in the world (Matthew 28:16–20; 1 John 4:6–8; John 3:16–17; Romans 8:28–29; Acts 2–3). This Lutheran evangelistic movement in the country of Haiti, West Indies, has proven the effectiveness of the Gospel's power when preached, modeled, communicated, and joyously proclaimed in purity and truth.

The models of church planting used over the twenty-five year history of the church in Haiti are unique. The theologically trained clergy have developed partnerships with North American Lutheran churches, institutions, and organizations for the purpose of fulfilling the Great Commission of the Lord Jesus Christ and expanding His kingdom in the world. This is achievable through:

- intentional strategic planning for the country of Haiti;

- sacrificial commitment of clergy, lay staff, teachers, and evangelists;

- total reliance on the Holy Scripture and the Holy Spirit;

97

• commitment to wipe out Voodoo worship in the country; and

• reliance on the Divine Word and Sacraments (Baptism and Holy Communion) as the mission and ministry foundation and evangelistic outreach.

Each of the professionally trained clergy is called to create new mission church plants and preaching stations in a strategic location. This is accomplished with God's Word, prayer, community outreach, evaluation of felt needs, leadership development, and evangelistic charisma.

A Short History of the Lutheran Church Development in Haiti

The Lutheran mission-church was started in 1980 in the City of Port au Prince, Haiti, with Pastor Doris Jean Louis. From 1980 to 1992, only four churches were planted in this one geographical area of the country. In 1992 Pastor Israel Izidor, a vicar under Pastor Louis, went to the city of Les Cayes and planted one mission-church with his family. By 1998 he was able to plant more than thirty churches in and around the city of Les Cayes. In order to manage these churches effectively and train more leaders, he opened a missionary training center. The center was structured and organized to train laymen and laywomen to be missionaries, teachers, church planters, and lay pastors for the ministry they were doing in Les Cayes. The more churches they planted, the more lay pastors were needed. By the year 2001 they had more than 150 churches, missions, and schools.

To start a church, various types of support are needed. Some of the needs include: a place to worship and money to rent a room(s), buy chairs, tables, pay utilities, and underwrite a stipend for the lay assistants. Church planters are expected to provide money for hymnals, Bibles, chairs, tables, and worship elements. In the beginning everything comes from the church planter.

Church planters must hold on to the Word of God. The base of the church is God's Word. His Word promises to guide us to the perfect things. "The heart of man plans his way, but the LORD establishes his steps" (Proverbs 16:9). We need laypeople who are capable of taking responsibility in the church. In the New Testament era, the Spirit of God used gifted men and women for management and administration of the life of the church of Jesus Christ (Romans 12:8; 1 Corinthians 12:28).

In Haiti, when we plant a church, we provide opportunities for other people to be involved in the work of Christ. They help others to move away from the bad spirits that are present in the country of Haiti. When we plant a church close to a Voodoo temple, they can no longer call the bad spirits, but have to move and go somewhere else. This is one of our prime objectives in church planting throughout the country.

Since 1992 there are churches, schools, mission stations, medical clinics, orphanages, and a variety of outreach ministries in nine strategically planned locations throughout the cities, towns, and countryside of Haiti. The approximate membership is well over forty thousand souls and the number continues growing rapidly. Eight ordained clergy presently lead the ministry, with five vicars, and over 300 lay preachers ministering throughout the country.

Church Planting in Haiti

We need the presence of the Holy Spirit to lead, guide, and direct every aspect of church planting. The first essential aspect is the preaching and teaching of the Word of God. In order for a sinner, a person who has no personal relationship with Jesus Christ, to receive Christ's gift of salvation, he or she needs to hear the Word of God so the Holy Spirit can persuade and convince. This unexplainable act is what the church and church planting is all about. The church is not our church, it is the church of Jesus Christ. He has redeemed the church by His death, resurrection, and the pouring out of His precious blood on the cross.

In the country of Haiti it is very easy to plant a new mission church because people are very open, free, and willing to listen. In addition, they have time to hear the Gospel, and faith comes from hearing the powerful Word of God.

The following are illustrations that are being used today by the pastoral leadership and church developers. This church-planting model is growing, and although currently it is underdeveloped, it is guided by the Holy Spirit.

Illustration A

A group of Christians can go out, where people are gathered, especially in an area where most of the people are poor. The people will immediately gather around you and allow you to talk to them for as long as you desire.

You will need to show them how extremely difficult life can be here on the earth. You must talk about the physical needs, emotional and spiritual problems of life. In addition you must let them know at the same time they have a greater need, which is a spiritual need. The greater need directly deals with their souls and their eternal future. It is important to inform them that one day they will have to come to God for the eternal judgment of their souls. The goal is to get them to understand that they can have eternal life with Christ forever in eternity. The Holy Spirit convinces them through the Word of God, brings them into a personal relationship with Christ, and they are saved from eternal punishment.

Illustration B

You must have musical instruments, musicians, a group of singers, an organizer, and a preacher to go into a targeted area. When you choose a particular location to play music and to sing, you need to be prepared for many people to come out to listen. The people have time and are free because many do not have jobs or other pressing obligations. The majority of the people of Haiti are unemployed. They will stop to listen, and many times join in with the singers in song or dance. In twenty to twenty-five minutes you will be surrounded by a big crowd of men, women, and children of all ages. From this group, about ten to twenty people will be converted and want a relationship with Christ; therefore you may consider planting a new church for these new Christian members. If you do not have any Lutheran Christians or churches close by, begin group meetings with small devotional worship services, Bible study, prayer hours, and fellowship gatherings. It is important to encourage the new Christians to invite other people who will want to join them for worship services, Bible studies, prayer meetings, and fellowship gatherings.

Illustration C

You will need qualified people to come into the targeted area and to work with the new Christians. Devotional worship services, prayer meetings, Bible studies, and fellowship gatherings need to be handled by trained laypeople or clergy. The people will need to be instructed in Lutheran doctrines (fundamental doctrines). In this way they will become Lutheran by faith, and when they become Lutheran by faith they will never turn away from the truth. They will know the voice of God; they will not follow the false prophets and Voodoo priests anymore. This is the reason why there is a great need to plant more churches.

Illustration D

We can use schools to plant new churches. We evangelize children and teachers in this model. Because we are targeting schools, we need qualified people to go and begin the mission. We need to use people depending on their qualifications and their spiritual gifts, not only those acting out of blind faith. When children hear the Gospel, they will bring many others who want to come and hear the Good News of Christ's salvation for all people.

An Informative Approach for Church Planting in Haiti

Getting to know the people in the community and allowing them to know us is another very important key to church planting in Haiti. We need to have personal contact with local people; the pastor or church planter must first become familiar with the people—know and be known—so the people will come to the church-planting events. Talk to the people and invite them to your new church-mission. You must work in such a way that rejuvenates existing churches while using their talents to reach out in many ways. In Haiti, when you plant a church, you may wait for a great success in numbers, but the strategy should always involve the formation of a dynamic church. Live your life for others, even though it is very hard, instead of living for yourself. Take care of others; you must be sensitive in Haiti to feel the immense social needs of the community and reach out to people in true Christian love and concern. To really understand the people in Haiti, work with them, understand their cultures, customs, traditions, and ethnicity.

Church Planting Is Not Church Affiliation

God sent us into the world (Matthew 28:19–20; Mark 16:15) to preach, teach, and to make disciples; so anytime someone comes to faith in Christ, we celebrate with a feast in heaven with the angels. With the new converts and those who were Christians for a long time, we plant a church and call it church planting. This is another model that is successfully used in Haiti. Faith in Christ means God gives you a new heart and a new spirit. Jesus replaces the heart of stone with a heart filled with His Spirit (Ezekiel 36:26).

We plant a new church with God's people, those who have been transformed as the Bible says: "Therefore, if anyone is in Christ, he is a new creation. The old has passed away; behold, the new has come" (2 Corinthians 5:17). Church planting is a way to reach the lost, especially in a community in which the church (Christians) is already planted. Wherever there is a plan to plant a new Lutheran church, there is a need for education and instruction in the fundamental doctrines of the church. The people or members who attend need to have those who will help them grow in Christ. Church planters must possess many spiritual gifts. They must have a deep passion for sharing their Spirit-given ability for Christian service. Through prayer meetings, Bible studies, worship services, and meetings, members work together to bring about the future of this new congregation.

Why Plant a New Church?

Why plant a church? Because, as people of God, we need to worship God. Jesus said, "[W]here two or three are gathered in My name, there am I among them" (Matthew 18:20). We plant a church to bring new and old believers together to worship God, practice our faith, and maintain our obedience to the essence of the Christian faith. The leader should be someone the group respects and who is willing to give the many hours necessary to sustain the life of the church.

Whoever is called to plant a church must have the ability to get people to come to worship. Many people want to have a church close by to attend for worship, Bible study, and fellowship activities. In Haiti many older people are willing to go to church, but they do not have transportation, perhaps because there are no buses in the area where they are living. A community church plant can be a tremendous blessing to those living in the area.

As people of God, and being human, we need to have a local church for worship, fellowship, and to develop a supportive community. It is a way to make people hear more about the Gospel, grow in their Christian faith, and share the message of salvation with others.

In Haiti, we plant many new churches to fight against Voodoo. When we plant a church, the Voodoo priests will have to leave because the power of the Gospel moves them away. Our power is from God, and He is more powerful than the evil that is connected with Voodoo.

We strategize to plant churches in Haiti because in many places people have a real need for communities of faith. Many of them have to walk more than fifty to sixty minutes to find a church to worship God on Sunday. It is hard to take children and older people this distance. Communities of faith, church plants, allow every person to hear the Word of God just like other people.

We need to plant churches because Haitian people are eager to hear the Good News of the Gospel. Many of them have tried Voodoo or Satan many times, but it did not work; therefore they really want to experience life with God. And the God we offer them is a God of grace, mercy, peace, joy, love, and eternal salvation. Oh, what a wonderful God He is!

We need to plant new Lutheran churches because we are servants of God and have been called to do so. We need to plant Lutheran churches because we need to preach the pure Gospel, to provide confession and absolution, and to administer the Sacraments. These churches will also teach the people about Holy Communion, and especially that communicants receive the body and blood of Jesus Christ in, under, and with the bread and wine for the remission of sins. In Haiti, we cannot get this kind of pure truth and teaching anywhere else than from the scriptural Lutheran teaching and preaching. We need to plant Lutheran churches, teaching and administering the Sacrament of Holy Baptism as a means of God's grace for adults and children (Matthew 28:18; Acts 2:38–39; Mark 10:13–16). Other churches preach against infant Baptism, but people need to hear from God's Word that He joins even children to His family through this precious Sacrament of water and the Word.

The Holy Spirit has blessed this unique and effective church planting ministry with a church body of over forty thousand members. There is a vision among the leadership to reach one million nonbelievers with the Gospel by the five hundredth anniversary of the Reformation in 2017. May God bring this vision to fruition.

Basics for Emulation and Practice

Robert H. King
Fourth Vice-President, The Lutheran Church—Missouri Synod

Jesus Leads the Way

In all these approaches to ministry with specific people groups, Jesus Christ is the number one model for Christian outreach. Jesus attracted and helped people in many walks of life: fishermen, tax collectors, lawyers, Roman soldiers, Jewish celebrities, beggars, the blind, the deaf, the dumb, the lame, and notorious sinners and outcasts, as well as the self-righteous and righteous.

The greater portion of Jesus' ministry was addressed to the wants and needs of people. His response to their needs aimed to meet the ultimate need everyone has for salvation and spiritual satisfaction. Thus, in many instances, Christ used the people's own experiences to convey His message. In other cases, Christ employed Old Testament prophecies and related how they were being fulfilled in the situations of that time.

Jesus spoke to people, but as an engaging orator and teacher, He brought His ideas to life through illustrations, rhythm, symbols, models, and real-life subject aids. If we were to analyze Christ's pedagogical approach, we could safely say that He used the deductive method of going from the known to the unknown, from the human to the divine, from prophecy to fulfillment, from temporal to spiritual, and from earthly to heavenly. He did not always teach people in the temple and synagogue. He taught them wherever opportunity presented itself and where people lived their lives—by the seashore, on the mountain, in the desert, in homes, at the marketplace, and by the well. There was no set time for holding teaching sessions, no class schedule.

Because most of His waking hours were spent with people, Jesus met with followers morning, afternoon, evening, and night, whenever teaching was sought or needed. His class sizes ranged all the way from one person to a reported five thousand, exclusive of women and children.

When Christ had completed three years of successful ministry, including His redemptive work on the cross and His triumphant resurrection, He turned over the work of God's kingdom to His devoted disciples. As He was about to ascend into heaven, Christ commanded His followers: "Go therefore and make disciples of all nations, baptizing them . . . teaching them . . ." (Matthew 28:19–20).

The mission began ten days later, on the first Christian Pentecost, when the Holy Spirit enabled the apostles to speak of the great works of God to the crowds from the corners of the Roman Empire gathered in Jerusalem. To the amazement of these international people, each heard the message in his or her own language. Some three thousand persons responded to the proclamation, were baptized, and became Christians. From all indications, these new converts together with the apostles, teachers, preachers, evangelists, elders, and other consecrated laymen carried on the work of Christ in Judea, Galilee, Samaria, Macedonia, and other near and faraway places.[1]

The important ascension directive to be witnesses to Christ has sounded and resounded to His followers down through nearly twenty centuries. We are to be His witnesses in figurative Jerusalems, Judeas, Samarias, and to the ends of the earth. In the United States, we have numerous thousands of representatives of diverse nations, cultures, languages, lifestyles, and religions of the world as objects of and for our witnessing. We have the opportunity for a contemporary Christian Pentecost with a myriad of people from around the world to whom we can declare the crucified and resurrected Savior and Lord.

A unique example of reaching out to witness to the world is the Ablaze initiative by The Lutheran Church—Missouri Synod and more than twenty partner church bodies around the globe. Ablaze is a worldwide initiative endeavoring to reach 100 million uncommitted or unreached persons by

---

[1] Robert King, "Implications for Adult Education in the Church," *Lutheran Education* (December 1970): 138–45.

the 500th anniversary of the Lutheran Reformation in 2017. The chief and focal words are:

One Mission—Seeking to save the lost sinner;

One Message—Jesus Christ is the only way to salvation; and

One People—All who believe are members of one family in Christ.

With 150 million unchurched people in the United States, congregations are called to action in reaching out to all people of the world with the Gospel, which is the power of God "for salvation to everyone who believes" (Romans 1:16). As Jesus said to Nicodemus, "For God so loved the world, that He gave His only Son, that whoever believes in Him should not perish but have eternal life" (John 3:16). This message of hope Paul rephrased as follows, "[Christ] died for all, that those who live might no longer live for themselves but for Him who for their sake died and was raised" (2 Corinthians 5:15).

OUTREACH IDEAS

In his book *264 Great Outreach Ideas*, Joel Heck focuses on two primary topics: (1) the Word of God and the church's ministry of salvation by Jesus Christ, and (2) the unique needs of community people, to which faithful people of the church respond through outreach, in keeping with God's strong Word.

According to Heck, the following are some general methods individuals can use to reach out or some places where witness might naturally occur:

Conversation	Personal invitation
Friendship	Lifestyle
Hospitality	Distribution of periodicals
The marketplace	Prayer
Meeting a need	Visits to the sick, shut-in,
Storytelling	and hospitalized
Times of transition	Distribution of tracts, tapes,
Cross-cultural setting	booklets, and brochures
Distribution of	Personal witness
foreign-language materials	

Following are some of Heck's fifty-two suggestions for personal witnessing:

1. Ask the Lord to guide you.
2. Ask Him to help you recognize what He's doing in your life.
3. Ask Him to loosen your tongue so you'll be able to talk about God in your life without embarrassment.
4. Let people see your joy in the Lord (not how good you are!).
5. Search the Word. How did Jesus win people? Peter? Paul?
6. Volunteer to call on newcomers or radio and television referrals.
7. Let your home declare the glory of God: pictures, plaques, posters, banners—all can harmonize with your decor.
8. Use greeting cards with a Christ-centered message.
9. Don't be a neatnik. Leave your church bulletin on the coffee table.
10. Watch your neighborhood for newcomers. Be the first to call on them with a plate of cookies.
11. When you dine out, leave a tract along with a generous tip.
12. When paying bills, enclose a tract with each check.
13. Asking God's guidance, make a list of those who seem to be outside the kingdom.
14. Pray for them.
15. Love them.
16. Seek their company. Invite them over for coffee (or appropriate beverage).
17. Ask God to prepare their hearts.
18. Ask God for (a) the opportunity to speak about spiritual things; (b) the discernment to recognize it; (c) the courage to speak; (d) the wisdom to say enough, but not too much.
19. Listen to them. Listen to them. Listen to them.
20. Watch for opportunities to let them tell you about their religious background.
21. Tell them yours, being sure to give God all the credit.
22. Invite your witnessees to a regular or special church service, a Bible study group, a fellowship event, or the adult information class.
23. If children are involved, offer to bring them to Sunday School or vacation Bible school.

24. Try to arrange for prospects to meet other members of your church.

25. Thank and praise God for opportunities to do all of the above.[2]

LEADERSHIP

Several vital principles are essential for productive leadership, with prime importance for outreach ministry to minorities. Key recognizable characteristics of leaders are listed below.

Cares for people	A servant and a follower
Listens	Willing to turn loose
An encourager	Not intimidated by smart people
A person who prays	Will establish goals
Learns by example	Will identify a successor[3]
Readily admits mistakes	

From firsthand experience as a professional adult educator and lay ministry trainer, I affirm flexible leadership roles and the following functions of effective leaders as teachers.

Catalyst	Role model
Expert	Provider
Facilitator	Servant
Friend	Stimulator
Helper	Transplanter of knowledge
Informer	Mentor
Initiator	Advisor
Instructor	Counselor
Leader	Communicator
Motivator	Empathizer
Practitioner	Substitute parent

Another requirement for effective leaders is for them to be servants in their ministry to people. Servant leadership is vital for Christlikeness in reaching out and connecting with other people.

---

[2] Reprinted from *264 Great Outreach Ideas* by Joel D. Heck © 1993 CPH. Used with permission.

[3] Wendell Haubein, "A True Leader Is a Teacher," in *Leadership: Maps, Models, and Morals*, compiled by Elena Vanalle Jungmeyer and Peter Kurowski (n.p.), 64–71. Used with permission.

- Humble themselves and wait for God to exalt them (Luke 14:7–11);
- Follow Jesus rather than seek a position (Mark 10:32–40);
- Give up personal rights to find greatness in the service of others (Mark 10:42–45);
- Can risk serving others because they trust that God is in control of their lives (John 13:3);
- Take up Jesus' towel of servanthood to meet the needs of others (John 13:4–11);
- Share their responsibility and authority with others to meet a greater need (Acts 6:1–7); and
- Multiply their leadership by empowering others to lead (Exodus 18:17–23).[4]

STEWARDSHIP

Servants of Christ who are involved in outreach ministry are to be His stewards, giving their time, their abilities, their gifts, and themselves in doing the Lord's kingdom work. To be effective stewards, they must be found faithful (1 Corinthians 4:1–2; Titus 1:7; 1 Peter 4:10). Meaningful incentives and directives are given in the following stewardship principles.

God's Stewards Are *God's* Stewards

This means that "God's stewards are stewards by virtue of creation and their recreation in Holy Baptism; therefore, they belong to the Lord."

God's Stewards Are Managers, Not Owners

This means that "God's stewards have been entrusted by God with life and life's resources and given the privilege of responsibly and joyfully managing them for Him."

God's Stewards Are Saints and Sinners

This means that "God's stewards rejoice in and live out what God has declared them to be through the cross. At the same time His stewards recognize they are sinners who fight sin and its consequences each day."

---

[4] Samuel Pourell, "Servant Leadership," in *Leadership: Maps, Models, and Morals*, compiled by Elena Vanalle Jungmeyer and Peter Kurowski (n.p.), 75. Used with permission.

God's Stewards Are Uniquely Singular, Yet Profoundly Plural

This means that "God's stewards recognize that their lives are not solo performances but are personal responses to God, lived out within the community of faith to benefit the whole world."

God's Stewards Are *in* the World, but Not *of* the World

This means that "God's stewards recognize that the Lord sets them apart from the world and by the transforming power of the Gospel sends them into the world to live out the Gospel."

God's Stewards Are Loved and Loving

This means that "God's stewards recognize that their stewardship flows out of God's act of love for them in Christ, which empowers them, in turn, to love others in acts of Christlike love."

God's Stewards Are Served and Serving

This means that "God's stewards recognize that their stewardship involves a Gospel-powered style of life which is demonstrated in servant-hood within all the arenas of life."

God's Stewards Live with an Awareness of the Present and Future, of Time and Eternity

This means that "God's stewards live intentionally in the light of God's eternal purpose while being firmly committed to His rule in the here and now."[5]

---

[5] These Biblical Stewardship Principles and the quoted meanings of each statement were presented at the 1998 LCMS Convention by the Biblical Stewardship Principles Task Force. See *Convention Workbook 1998* (St. Louis: LCMS, 1998), 293–96.

Congregations Reaching

Robert H. King
Fourth Vice-President, The Lutheran Chuch—Missouri Synod

This book concludes with suggestions for training laypersons for Christian mission. Many congregations use the talents of laity, even for outreach ministries. Nevertheless, we want to sensitize laity to the impact of their actions on others, based on Alan F. Harre's schema. In short, Harre reminds us that the productive intentions of active members may unintentionally trigger or beget feelings of victimization with inactive members.

How Church Members See and Feel (Labels, Stereotypes, Barriers, and Misunderstandings)

Active Members

How They See Inactives	How They Feel toward Inactives
Dropouts	Frustrated
Delinquents	Fearful
Do-nothings	Anxious
Inactive	Worried
Lazy	Hostile
Backsliders	Suspicious
Sinners	Full of Pity
Complainers	Sympathetic
Excuse Makers	Puzzled
Embarrassed	

Inactive Members

How They See Actives	How They Feel toward Actives
Hypocrites	Condemned
Do-Gooders	Forgotten
Nosy	Left out
Fussy	Lonely
Nitpickers	Rejected
Bossy	Abandoned
"In group"	Angry
Judges	High and mighty
Meddlers[1]	

The two workshop models that follow may be used by congregations to review the effectiveness of lay outreach ministries to ethnic groups or individuals. The workshops also may be used to train laypeople for such ministries or to strengthen participation by all church members (new, long-time, of any ethnicity) and encourage Christlike compassion as we reach out to those who do not know the Good News of salvation in Christ. The Holy Spirit will work through God's Word and the Sacraments to achieve effective witness internally and externally—reducing backdoor losses and opening wide the front doors to new members of all cultures.

The workshop models that follow are two of a series that I designed and that were implemented on thirty occasions in six LCMS districts from 1987 to 1990.

---

[1] Reprinted from *Close the Back Door* by Alan F. Harre © 1984 CPH. Used with permission.

Workshop on Lay Ministry in the Church

Lay Ministry Training

One to three days in length

Goal

To establish and administer real-life basic programs that will enable the church to identify and use the resources of pastors and laity to minister more effectively.

Objectives

1. To provide opportunities for pastors to develop communication and nurturing skills that will result in more laypeople being equipped for and involved in the mission and ministry of the church.

2. To provide opportunities for pastors to discover, develop, and use time, talents, and treasures that will help fulfill the mission and ministry of the church.

Description

A workshop to sensitize pastors and laypeople to the need to use and develop the gifts and skills of laypeople in the ministry and mission of the church.

Principal Units

I. Biblical and Theological Principles for Lay Ministry in the Church

    A. The church is the body of Christ (Romans 12:5; 1 Corinthians 12:27).

B. Members of the church have numerous spiritual gifts, roles, and functions (1 Corinthians 12).

C. Members of the church are to be equipped saints in fulfilling their high calling in Jesus Christ (Ephesians 4:4–7, 11–16).

D. Theological "jewels" of the Lutheran Reformation

    1. The open Bible (John 5:39; Matthew 22:37–39; 2 Timothy 3:13–17)

    2. Justification by faith (Romans 3:28; Romans 5:1)

    3. Freedom of conscience (1 Timothy 1:2, 19)

    4. Priesthood of all believers (1 Peter 2:9; Revelation 1:6)

    5. Universal Christian education (Deuteronomy 6:4–7; Ephesians 6:4; Matthew 28:19–20)

E. New Testament role models for current usages

    1. Samaritan woman at well—community ministry (John 4:27–30)

    2. Women after the resurrection—witnessing to other Christians (Luke 24:8–11)

    3. Stephen and associates—elders' ministry (Acts 6:1–6)

    4. Jailer at Philippi—household ministry (Acts 16:29–33)

    5. Philip and the Ethiopian—cross-cultural ministry (Acts 8:35–39)

6. Eunice and Lois—teaching the young (2 Timothy 1:5)

7. Lydia—household ministry (Acts 16:14–15)

8. Aquila and Priscilla—missionary, lay missionary (Romans 16:3; 1 Corinthians 16:19; 2 Timothy 4:19)

9. Cornelius—household ministry (Acts 10:31–42)

10. Dorcas—social ministry (Acts 9:36–42)

11. Peter in prison—prison ministry (Acts 12:50)

12. Other

II. Practical Principles for Lay Ministry of a Congregation

A. Functions of a congregation

1. Worship

2. Witness

3. Nurture

4. Service

5. Fellowship

B. "Called Out and Sent Back" (video)

C. Lay leadership roles and functions in a congregation

1. Elder or another approved officer or layperson

- serving as lector

- leading the liturgy

- lay reading of the sermon

- assisting with Communion

2. Other laypersons

- making hospital calls

- calling on inactive members

- assimilating new members

- welcoming visitors

- serving as ushers

- conducting group devotions

- conducting fellowship activities

- teaching Sunday School

- conducting a "prayer chain"

- helping with public relations, communications, media

- showing help to the poor, needy, and grieving

- using musical talents

- serving on stewardship committee

- serving on evangelism committee

- serving on other committees

• serving in LLL, LWML, ladies' aid, men's club, etc.

• helping with youth work, family ministry, etc.

Methods and/or Techniques

- Workshop—Type of meeting that offers opportunities for persons with a common interest or problem to meet with specialists to receive firsthand information and practice

- Mini-lectures—Carefully prepared short oral presentations of a subject by a qualified person

- Lecture or speech—Carefully prepared oral presentation of a subject by a qualified person

- Group discussion—Purposeful conversation and deliberation about a topic of mutual interest among six to twenty participants under the guidance of a trained leader

- Audio-visual tools—Aids that assist in the learning process through the employment of more than one of the senses

- Demonstration—Carefully prepared presentation that shows how to perform an act or use a procedure

- Role-play—Spontaneous portrayal (acting out) of a situation or circumstance by selected members of the learning group

- Forum—Period of open discussion—often 15 to 60 minutes—in which the entire group is able to question one or more resource persons

Church-Planting Workshop

Lay Ministry Training

One to three days in length

Goal

To establish and administer real-life basic programs that will enable the church to identify and use the resources of pastors and laity to minister more effectively.

Objectives

1. To provide opportunities for pastors to develop communication and nurturing skills that will result in more laypeople being equipped for and involved in the mission and ministry of the church.

2. To provide opportunities for pastors and/or laity to study how to plant missions and how different styles of worship can result in meaningful and effective worship.

Description

A workshop to sensitize pastors and laypeople to the need to use and develop the gifts and skills of laypeople in the ministry and mission of the church.

Principal Units

I. Biblical and Theological Principals for Lay Church Planting

A. The Great Commission (Matthew 28:18–20; Mark 16:15–16; Acts 1:8)

B. The Great Commission in church-planting theology

　　1. Only God can make a church (Matthew 16:18)

　　2. Method, mandate, and means

　　3. The Great Commission in church planting: How it works

　　4. What it means, in the response to the Great Commission

C. The body of Christ in church-planting theology (Ephesians 4:15–16)

　　1. How it works

　　2. Your pattern for your new living church will include certain identifiable features

　　3. How you grow

D. "The Pauline cycle"[2]

　　• Step 1: Missionaries commissioned (Acts 13:1–4; 15:39–40)

　　• Step 2: Audience contacted (Acts 13:24–16; 14:1)

　　• Step 3: Gospel communicated (Acts 13:17ff; 16:31)

　　• Step 4: Hearers converted (Acts 13:48; 16:14–15)

　　• Step 5: Believers congregated (Acts 13:43)

---

[2] This model for church planting is suggested by David J. Hesselgrave in his book, *Planting Churches Cross-Culturally* (Grand Rapids: Baker, 1980). He posits that this model has been used from the beginning of the church age until now and attests to its successful implementation.

• Step 6: Faith confirmed (Acts 14:21–22; 15:41)

• Step 7: Leadership consecrated (Acts 14:23)

• Step 8: Believers commended (Acts 14:23; 16:40)

• Step 9: Relationship continued (Acts 15:36; 18:23)

• Step10: Sending churches convened (Acts 15:26–27; 15:1–4)

Note: The Holy Spirit is the Divine Director of the missionary enterprise (Acts 13:2, 52); prayer begins the enterprise (Acts 13:1–4); the Scriptures are the foundation (Acts 15:15); the church is the agency (Acts 15:22)

E. "The Great Commission Church Planting Strategy" (Video)

II. Practical Principles for Lay Church Planting

A. Why plant new churches?

B. Some places and situations for planting churches

1. Starting a church in the inner-city

2. Starting a church in a low-rent housing project

3. Starting a church downtown

4. Starting a church in a shopping plaza or mall

5. Starting a church on a college or university campus

6. Starting a church in a resort area

7. Starting a church in a prison

8. Starting a church in suburbia

9. Starting a church in an apartment complex or village

10. Starting a church in a rural community

11. Starting a church in a mobile unit or facility

12. Starting a church in a home for the elderly

13. Starting a church through street ministry

14. Starting a church through media ministry

15. Starting churches geared to specific ethnic groups such as African American, Chinese, Hispanic, Korean, Vietnamese, Cuban, Indian, Caucasian, Japanese, Jewish, or others

C. Ways to establish new congregations

1. Arises more or less spontaneously

2. Through a circuit forum or cluster of congregations

3. By a Sunday School or home Bible class

4. By a congregation starting a second- or third-language congregation

5. By an established congregation starting a daughter congregation

6. By an established congregation starting a satellite congregation

7. By a synodical district starting a new mission in a strategic location

D. Worship plan for beginning a church

1. Scripturally centered worship

2. In keeping with Lutheran doctrine and the Lutheran Confessions

3. "Voices of Resurrection" (video)

4. Considerations for the new mission situation:

- the community

- the group

- the maturity of the group

- the finances

- the commitment to the Lord

Methods and/or Techniques

- Workshop—Type of meeting that offers opportunities for persons with a common interest or problem to meet with specialists to receive firsthand information and practice

- Mini-lectures—Carefully prepared short oral presentations of a subject by a qualified person

- Lecture or speech—Carefully prepared oral presentation of a subject by a qualified person

- Group discussion—Purposeful conversation and deliberation about a topic of mutual interest among six to twenty participants under the guidance of a trained leader

- Audio-visual tools—Aids that assist in the learning process through the employment of more than one of the senses

- Demonstration—Carefully prepared presentation that shows how to perform an act or use a procedure

- Role-play—Spontaneous portrayal (acting out) of a situation or circumstance by selected members of the learning group

- Forum—Period of open discussion—often 15 to 60 minutes—in which the entire group is able to querstion one or more resource persons

- Question period—Period of a meeting—often 5 to 20 minutes—in which the group may ask questions of a speaker or other resource person

- Simulation—Role-playing specific scenarios with the intent of imitating best practices

Have this mind among yourselves, which is yours in *Christ Jesus*, who, though He was in the form of God, did not count *equality with God* a thing to be grasped, but made Himself nothing, taking the form of a *servant*, being born in the *likeness of men*. And being found in human form, He humbled Himself by becoming *obedient to the point of death*, even death on a cross. Therefore God has highly exalted Him and bestowed on Him the name that is above every name, so that at the name of Jesus *every knee should bow*, in heaven and on earth and under the earth, and every tongue *confess that Jesus Christ is Lord*, to the glory of God the Father. (Philippians 2:5–11)

Soli Deo Gloria!